Forming the Church in the Modern World

The Theological Contributions of Avery Cardinal Dulles, SJ

EDITED BY THOMAS A. BAIMA

Paulist Press
New York / Mahwah, NJ

Cover image by WenPhotos / Pixabay.com
Cover design by Tamian Wood
Book design by Sharyn Banks

Library of Congress Cataloging-in-Publication Data

Names: Baima, Thomas A., editor.
Title: Forming the church in the modern world : the theological contributions of Avery Cardinal Dulles, SJ / edited by Thomas A. Baima.
Description: New York : Paulist Press, [2019] | "The Introduction and chapters 1 to 6 have previously been published by Chicago Studies and have been adapted, updated, and reprinted with permission from the Civitas Dei Foundation. The conclusion "From Convert to Cardinal" by Anne-Marie Kirmse, OP was originally published as "Avery Dulles: From Convert to Cardinal" in Here Comes Everybody: Catholic Studies in American Higher Education, pages 158–169, edited by William C. Graham and has been adapted, updated, and reprinted with permission from University Press of America, a member of the Rowman & Littlefield Group"—T.p. verso. | Includes bibliographical references and index.
Identifiers: LCCN 2018029766 (print) | LCCN 2018041639 (ebook) | ISBN 9781587688041 (e-book) | ISBN 9780809154234 (pbk. : alk. paper)
Subjects: LCSH: Dulles, Avery, 1918–2008. | Catholic Church—Liturgy—Theology. | Church—History of doctrines—20th century. | Catholic Church—Doctrines—History—20th century.
Classification: LCC BX4705.D867 (ebook) | LCC BX4705.D867 F67 2019 (print) | DDC 230/.2092—dc23
LC record available at https://lccn.loc.gov/2018029766

ISBN 978-0-8091-5423-4 (paperback)
ISBN 978-1-58768-804-1 (e-book)

Published by Paulist Press
997 Macarthur Boulevard
Mahwah, New Jersey 07430

www.paulistpress.com

Printed and bound in the United States of America

This book is dedicated to my predecessors,
the Academic Deans of Mundelein Seminary

The Reverend John B. Furay, SJ
1922–41

The Reverend John J. Clifford, SJ
1942–54

The Reverend Joseph M. Egan, SJ
1955–59

The Reverend Bernard McMann, SJ
1960–65

The Very Reverend William La Sainte, SJ
1966–69

The Reverend George Dyer
1969–77

The Reverend Charles R. Meyer
1977 (acting)
1978–81

The Reverend Edward Stokes, SJ
1981–85

The Reverend John G. Lodge
1985–89

The Reverend Gorman Sullivan, OCarm
1989–92

The Reverend Martin A. Zielinski
1992–98

The Reverend John G. Lodge
1998–2003

The Reverend Raymond J. Webb
2003–11

Any aggiornamento that [the Council] accomplished was intrinsically connected with the principle of *ressourcement*. "Every renewal of the Church" for the Council, "essentially consists in an increase of fidelity to her own calling" (*UR* 6).

Avery Cardinal Dulles, SJ

CONTENTS

PREFACE

It was a pleasure to participate in the symposium on Cardinal Dulles's work....You will be happy to learn that Cardinal Dulles kept the issue of *Chicago Studies* that featured the talks given at that symposium on his tray table from the time he received it until the morning he died. Although he was unable to hold a book any longer nor turn the pages, his former students came and read the articles aloud to him. He was so pleased with what had been said during the symposium.

Anne-Marie Kirmse, OP, PhD
Assistant to the late Avery Cardinal Dulles
Research Associate
Laurence J. McGinley Chair in Religion and Society
Fordham University

ACKNOWLEDGMENTS

A book such as this has a long and invisible history. Authors' and editors' names appear on the cover and in databases, but that short entry fails to acknowledge the community of persons who each individually contributed to such a book.

This book, and each of the others I have published since becoming an administrator, goes back to a dare. I was named to the faculty of Mundelein Seminary in 2000. Eight months later, I became provost. At that time, I was speaking to my colleague in Catholic-Jewish relations, Rabbi Dr. Byron Sherwin, the dean of Spertus Institute of Jewish Leadership and Learning. I expressed to him how many people had told me that the administrative appointment was the end of my academic writing and publishing. Dr. Sherwin replied that his friends had told him the same thing. He resolved to be both a scholar and administrator, excelling at both. He exhorted me to "prove them wrong, over and over again." He did this himself by publishing at least sixteen books. This is my seventh book as I try to live up to that exhortation.

For the present work, I must acknowledge the community of the University of Saint Mary of the Lake and especially Mundelein Seminary. My thanks go especially to its Chancellor, Cardinal Blase J. Cupich, archbishop of Chicago, who has consistently affirmed me in my intellectual apostolate.

Another important context for my work has been the Northside Chicago Theological Institute. This consortium of five theological seminaries has provided me with the opportunity to teach two seminars each year with faculty colleagues from the Association of Chicago Theological Schools. I have learned so much from listening to their lectures and dialoguing with them in the seminars. I appreciate especially the collaboration I have shared with the late Dr. Richard W. Carlson, Dr. Richard Cook, Dr. Elizabeth Y. Sung, Dr. Harold Netland, Rev. Norma Sutton, Dr. Paul Koptek, and Dr. David Bjorlin. They, too, are partners in this work.

I am also shaped in my scholarship by my relationship with the Institute of Ecumenical Studies at the Ukrainian Catholic University. The annual course I codirected with Professor Dr. Heleen Zorgdrager of the Protestant Theological University of the Netherlands connects me with students from many parts of the world.

During the period of this book's formation, I was fortunate to have a fellowship at the Shalom Hartman Institute in Jerusalem. I am especially grateful to Rabbi Dr. Rachel Sabath Beit-Halachmi, Dr. Marcie Lenk, Rabbi Noam Marans, and Emily Soloff for their assistance in the Hartman program. The year-long Christian Leadership Initiative, cosponsored by the American Jewish Committee and Hartman, brought Christian professors and seminary educators together for intensive study. These relationships continue to be part of the academic context that I bring to my work.

Of course, when you have written and compiled a book manuscript, the task is only about one-quarter finished. In that phase, each author and contributor is a partner in the final product. I am grateful to the authors, Father Aidan Nichols, Msgr. Paul McPartlan, Bishop Robert Barron, Father Edward T. Oakes, SJ, Father Emery de Gaál, Father Raymond Webb, and Sister Anne-Marie Kirmse, OP, who are more fully identified in the contributor page for their scholarship and willingness to participate in the various phases of this project. I owe a great debt to Natalie Jordan, my graduate assistant, whose expertise in editing perfected the manuscript for submission. I also wish to thank my colleague, Kevin Thornton, for his support for the project and his expertise at guiding me through the publication process. Special thanks go to Paul McMahon, my editor at Paulist Press, who ultimately made this book a reality.

This book project extends two other projects related to these texts. Each of the contributors were participants in the Albert Cardinal Meyer Lecture Series at Mundelein Seminary. My thanks go to the Meyer Lecture Committee for that series, especially Msgr. John F. Canary, Father

Raymond J. Webb, Father John Lodge, Dr. Joan Meyer Anzia, and Francis Cardinal George. I also must mention Bonnie Pijut, my administrative assistant when I was in the Office of the Provost, who handled the details of the Dulles colloquium, and Mary Bertram, my administrative assistant in the Office of Academic Affairs, who largely manages the details of the Meyer Lectures. The second phase of each lecture series is the publication of the lectures in abridged form in the journal *Chicago Studies*. I am grateful to the editors of that issue, Father Lawrence Hennessey and Father Michael J. K. Fuller, for their good work on the project and for the permission from the Civitas Dei Foundation to publish the full texts of the essays. I also thank Roman and Littlefield for the permission to include Sister Anne-Marie Kirmse's essay.

Mundelein Seminary is a rare setting for a professor. Because it has a largely residential faculty, with a common table for professors, there is a much higher level of intellectual exchange than in other universities. Living together and eating together daily should earn us a few semester hours of credit each year. I have benefited much from the informal, but nonetheless demanding, conversations at table.

No one is an island. We depend on each other for support and love. I thank my family, my sister Judy, my brother-in-law, Bob, my nephews Steve and Chris, with his wife, Carter, and their children, Olivia and Gray. We are a small family, separated by thousands of miles, yet always close in our hearts. I also thank my "family by choice" the Butler Group, who have accompanied me through the years.

This book is also my testimony to the vision and ministry of Francis Cardinal George, who originally conceived the notion of a symposium on the entire corpus of work by Avery Cardinal Dulles and was so supportive of all of us at Mundelein. May he rest in peace.

INTRODUCTION

Thomas A. Baima

More than any other text on the Church, Cardinal Dulles's most famous book, *Models of the Church*, shaped American ecclesiology for an entire generation of clergy, religious, and lay ecclesial ministers. While Cardinal Dulles wrote twenty-three books and over eight hundred articles, essays, and reviews in his lengthy career as a theologian, it is fair to say that this title is the one that comes to mind for most people when his name is mentioned. Hence, it has become a monument to his theology.

Models of the Church is also a window into his theological project. The use of modeling as an element of theological methodology runs throughout his career. Other titles such as *Models of Revelation*, employ the same approach.[1] Part of his theological project is to bring clarity to controversial questions by focusing on the distinctiveness of particular positions. While his use of this method would come to serve different purposes over the course of his career, it has remained a distinctive feature of his theology. This methodological point—the identification of distinctiveness—is something Cardinal Dulles contributed to the ecumenical movement, especially in the emerging new ecumenism of the last ten years.

Our examination of *Models of the Church* is in four parts. First, we will briefly describe the finding Cardinal Dulles reports from the use of this method in the first edition of *Models of the Church*. Second, we will examine modeling and its role in a theological methodology. Third, we will examine the development of his thought in the revision of the book for its expanded edition.[2] In this section, we will also

1

examine his development of a synthetic sixth model, the community of disciples. Finally, we will briefly comment on what Cardinal Dulles offers the ecumenical movement, and especially the new ecumenism.

MODELS OF THE CHURCH

Cardinal Dulles named five models that he hoped would enrich our understanding of the mystery of the Church. In this section, I will simply identify the five models and give Dulles's definition, usually in his own words. This material will become the foundation for the rest of our discussion.

The models are all presented in the form of the Church as "name of model." Thus, we have the Church as institution, mystical communion, sacrament, herald, and servant. In considering the Church as institution, Dulles writes,

> The Church is essentially a society—a perfect society in the sense that it is subordinate to no other and lacks nothing required for its own institutional completeness. Bellarmine affirmed that the Church is a society, "as visible and palpable as the community of the Roman people, or the kingdom of France, or the Republic of Venice."[3] The Church is described by analogies taken from political society.[4]

This model finds its basis in the theology of the Counter Reformation and in the canonical tradition. It was the official model of that same period and was enshrined in the theology of the First Vatican Council. In many ways, this first model was the one against which modern theologians were reacting in the development of ecclesiology that blossomed in the first half of the twentieth century.

The second model is the Church as mystical communion. Dulles points to the work of two French-speaking theologians, Yves Congar and Jerome Hamer, who developed this approach, based in part on new developments in the social sciences. Dulles writes,

Yves Congar and Jerome Hamer have made the category of community or communion central to their ecclesiology. Throughout the works of Congar one encounters the idea that the Church has two inseparable aspects. On the one hand, it is a fellowship of persons—a fellowship of men with God and with one another in Christ. On the other hand, the Church is also the totality of the means by which this fellowship is produced and maintained. In its former aspect the Church is *Heilsgemeinshaft* (community of salvation); in its latter aspect, *Heilsanstalt* (institution of salvation). In its ultimate reality, Congar says, the Church is a fellowship of persons.[5]

Dulles will later say that "the two models of Body of Christ and People of God both illuminate from different angles the notion of the Church as communion....The Church, from this point of view, is not in the first instance an institution or a visibly organized society. Rather, it is a communion of men, primarily interior but also expressed by external bonds of creed, worship and ecclesiastical fellowship."[6]

The third model of Church is based on the work of Henri de Lubac and Karl Rahner. It was then developed by Edward Schillebeeckx. This approach to the Church has deep patristic and medieval roots. The basic notion is well expressed by de Lubac in his magisterial work, *Catholicism*:

> If Christ is the sacrament of God, the church is for us the sacrament of Christ; she represents him, in the full and ancient meaning of the term, she really makes him present. She not only carries on his work, but she is his very continuation, in a sense far more real than that in which it can be said that any human institution is its founder's continuation.[7]

This theology would be later explored by another speaker at this Meyer Lecture Series, Father Paul McPartlan, whose book *The Eucharist Makes the Church* explores de Lubac's sacramental ecclesiology in depth.[8]

The fourth model is the Church as herald. It is distinguished from the third model by making "word primary and sacrament secondary."[9] Its

key insight is kerygmatic. Dulles identifies Richard McBrien as offering
the best statement of the model:

> This mission of the Church is one of proclamation of the
> word of God to the whole world. The Church cannot hold
> itself responsible for the failure of men to accept it as God's
> Word; it has only to proclaim it with integrity and persistence.
> All else is secondary. The church is essentially a kerygmatic
> community which holds itself aloft, through the preached
> Word, the wonderful deeds of God in past history, particularly
> his mighty act in Jesus Christ. The community itself happens
> wherever the Spirit breathes, wherever the Word is proclaimed
> and accepted in faith. The Church is an event, a point of
> encounter with God.[10]

This model owes its principal articulation to Karl Barth, the great
Protestant theologian of the early twentieth century.[11] Based on a reading
of Saint Paul and Luther, it is the dominant model found in Protestant
theology today.

Finally, we come to the fifth model, the Church as servant. This
is a complex model, based on a new theological methodology found in
the Pastoral Constitution on the Church in the Modern World,
Gaudium et Spes:

> The Pastoral Constitution on the Church in the Modern
> World, the most novel and distinctive contribution of Vatican
> II, outlines a completely new understanding of the relation-
> ship between the Church and the world of our day. It recog-
> nizes the "legitimate autonomy" of human culture and
> especially of the sciences, it calls upon the Church to update
> itself—including its doctrine and institutional structures—so
> as to appropriate the best achievements of modern secular life.
> It affirms that the Church must respect the accomplishments
> of the world and learn from them, lest it fall behind the times
> and become incapable of effectively heralding the gospel.
> Finally, it asserts that the Church should consider itself as part

of the total human family, sharing the same concerns as the
rest of men. Thus, in Article 3, after asserting that the Church
should enter into conversation with all men, the Constitution
teaches that just as Christ came into the world not to be
served but to serve, so the Church, carrying on the mission of
Christ, seeks to serve the world by fostering the brotherhood
of all men....The theological method accompanying this
type of ecclesiology differs from the more authoritarian
types...of past centuries...and may be called "secular-
dialogic": secular because the Church takes the world as a
properly theological locus, and seeks to discern the signs of
the times; dialogic, because it seeks to operate on the frontier
between the contemporary world and the Christian tradition...rather than simply apply the latter as the measure of the
former. The image of the Church that best harmonizes with
this attitude is that of Servant.[12]

While the herald model tends to be found in the conservative Protestant
communities, the servant model is dominant in the mainline communities.

As noted earlier, our goal was to understand his nomenclature and
to have the five models as a foundation for the rest of this study and its
consideration of the topics of ecclesiology and ecumenism. With this
summary of the findings of *Models of the Church*, let's now consider the
methodology.

METHODOLOGY

Methodology is an area of theology that is often neglected. Perhaps
my starting point stems from my original training in philosophy that
taught me always to begin any analysis by questioning the tacit presuppositions of an author, prior even to the engagement of his or her argument. In fact, it is especially appropriate since Avery Cardinal Dulles was
one of the American theologians who always paid close attention to
methodological questions. Indeed, the very idea of using models in theological work is a methodological move that followed him throughout his

intellectual career. Consequently, we will dwell on chapter one of *Models of the Church* where Cardinal Dulles explores the "Use of Models in Ecclesiology."[13]

Our two goals in this section are the following: first, to explore the idea of modeling as a method of theological reflection; and second, to examine the effect of Dulles's modeling exercise and its misuse by some of his readers.

Regarding modeling as a theological method, we recall what Msgr. Guido Pozzo wrote as he began his treatment of method in systematic theology:

> The doctrine of theological method is thus intended to expose the bases and presuppositions of theological knowledge with a view to showing the value of affirmations about theological reflection in general and that concerned with individual and specific contents of faith. Whereas theology is defined as a critical, methodical and systematic reflection on the faith of the church, reflection on method has for its object the study of the norms, criteria and operations that theology fulfills, for its theological activity to be carried out as it should.[14]

In *Models of the Church*, Dulles describes the sources of his method and his decision to use a modeling, or semiotic, approach to the subject.[15] The decision is rooted in semiotic theory.[16] Dulles writes,

> When an image is employed reflectively and critically to deepen one's theoretical understanding of a reality it becomes what is today called a "model." Some models are also images— that is, those that can be readily imagined. Other models are of a more abstract nature and are not precisely images. In the former class one might put temple, vine, and flock; in the latter, institution, society, community.[17]

Given the structure of *Lumen Gentium*, the Dogmatic Constitution on the Church, issued by the Second Vatican Council, which begins with the notion of the Church as mystery[18] and then explores that mystery through a survey of the images[19] that the sacred authors use to describe this divine-human reality in the pages of the Bible; the modeling approach seems to fit very well Pozzo's description of theology "defined [as] a critical, methodical and systematic reflection on the faith of the church."[20] But this is only the second half of the quotation. Pozzo also tells us that theological methodology seeks "for its object the study of the norms, criteria and operations that theology fulfills, for its theological activity to be carried out as it should."[21] Dulles was always attentive to this crucial point. Sadly, some of his readers are not, as will be discussed later.

In the first chapter of *Models of the Church,* Dulles quotes Professor Ewert Cousins's article "Models and the Future of Theology."[22] Professor Cousins, who was well known to Mundelein since he served as Chester and Margaret Paluch Professor of Theology in the early 2000s and was professor emeritus of theology at Fordham University, argues in that article for the employment of models as a way for theology to address the failure of the so-called secular theological method, which demythologized most of the sacred symbols of Christianity in favor of a scientific approach that, in the end, was reductionistic.[23] Cousins argues that modeling restores the mystery to theology by recognizing the inability of human language, even sacred language, to capture adequately the reality beneath the experience of mystery. He sees both the technological advances in information science and communications as opening humankind to a wider and less particular experience. The very wideness of this experience, which is enhanced by what we have come to call globalization, will demand of the theologian a language that opens up rather than closes down possibilities.

Models in mathematics and the physical sciences posit the vastness of reality against our ability to describe it in human language. So, the mathematician and scientist employ models as a way of describing part of a much greater and elusive whole. Cousins uses the example of light, which is sometimes best described as a wave and other times as a particle, but which is more than either description, to give us a hint of how theology could benefit from modeling as a descriptive method. Cousins writes,

> The widespread use of the model method at the present time
> is not a matter of chance, but rather grows out of our historical

situation. For the model method opens man to the complexity of the world. It is based on the assumption that reality is multi-dimensional and that there is a need for a variety of forms to reflect it. Since there is no need to use a single model for his vision of the world, the scientist can be open to the historical process and development. He does not have to freeze new developments with static forms. If another model will throw light on reality, he will use it. And in this on-going process, he always holds his models open to testing; they are hypotheses that must be verified and criticized in a number of ways. Thus the method has openness and flexibility but at the same time allows great precision and clarity. This set of qualities recommends the method for theology at the present time.[24]

Cousins goes on to describe how the scientific approach to models, both in the physical sciences and in the social sciences, offers a great deal to theology, especially in the way the models describe experience. There is a danger, which Cousins identifies, when

> the theologian may copy the sciences too closely. He may take the scientific method as a normative model, or he may so shape his use of the method that he emphasizes those aspects of theological models that most correspond to scientific models. In so doing, the theologian may not take into account the subjective element at the core of religion.[25]

We can follow Cousins's point about not allowing a scientific model to become an end in itself, especially as he has already warned us that models show their value precisely in the way they move us out of secular theological method. But the philosophy student in me asks another question: What is the object of study in this modeling method?

Returning to Pozzo's definition of *theological method*, we see that the object is what he terms "individual and specific contents of faith." These contents find their ground in "the bases and presuppositions of theological knowledge."[26] Here is one of the major concerns that will play itself out in the eventual reception of the book, and which eventually led Dulles to revise the book in the expanded edition.

While Dulles was careful through his ecclesiological writing to constantly call the reader back to the fact that Christianity is a revealed religion, there was, at the same time that he was writing, another approach that used the theory of religions popularized by the Chicago School to locate the basis of religion in experience.[27] Cousins represents this strand of thought.[28] In contrast to this approach, we find the New Yale School, developed principally by George Lindbeck and Hans Frei, that situates itself between experiential expressivism and the neoorthodoxy of Karl Barth on the question of religion.[29]

In conclusion, while the use of models is a legitimate and necessary enterprise in theology, the presuppositions about what is being modeled has a tremendous impact on the resulting theological product. Dulles makes a careful qualification of the normativity of revelation that we do not find in Cousins or his other sources. This stress on the normativity of revelation represents one of his contributions to theological methodology.

The second point regarding this now extended reflection on theological methodology relates to the effects of the modeling project on North American theology. Dulles wrote in 1974,

> By the exploratory, or heuristic, use of models, I mean their
> capacity to lead to new theological insights. This role is harder
> to identify, because theology is not an experimental science in
> the same way that physics, for example, is. Theology has an
> abiding objective norm in the past—that is, in the revelation
> that was given once and for all in Jesus Christ. There can be
> no other Gospel (cf. Gal. 1:8).[30]

In this important corrective to the danger, noted earlier, of an experiential expressive use of models, Dulles notes, but passes over another methodological problem, heuristics. In my work on doctrinal decision-making in American Protestant denominations, I argued that the presence of heuristics create traps for the theological enterprise.[31] To understand this point, let me first explain how a heuristic works.

The decision distortions I am referring to are a series of unconscious routines—popularly called "rules of thumb" and technically known as heuristics. The word *heuristic* is derived from the Greek: (*heuriskein*), which means "to discover" or "to find." In its Indo-European root *wer*, it has the same meaning and has given us another English word which perhaps better illustrates what is going on in this process, *eureka*.[32]

That is an apt description of how the routines work. They are shortcuts in decision-making, which, because they are unconscious, represent what Edward Russo and Paul Schoemaker have termed "decision traps."[33] Cognitive processes have been a darling of management scientists and students of organizations beginning in the final decade of the last century. This is an appropriate approach because decisions are not only the acts of individuals, but also of groups of individuals gathered into organizations. A congregation, parish, presbyterate, or even an entire ecclesial community are actors in decisions. In an analysis of how these unconscious routines effect the decision-making in ecumenical dialogues, I used the nomenclature developed by John Hammond, Ralph Keeney, and Howard Raiffa from their own study of heuristics in organizational decision-making. In most organizations, we can identify six such routines or decision traps:

1. The anchoring trap

2. The status-quo trap

3. The sunk-cost trap

4. The confirming-evidence trap

5. The framing trap

6. Estimating and forecasting traps[34]

Let us now describe each only insofar as they relate to the problem of the authentic reception of the Council. The reason for doing this here is not, first, to present on a treatise on cognitive science. Rather, it is to illustrate how the heuristic quality of models, while offering us important insights into the mystery of the Church, can also have unintended effects, shrinking instead of broadening our understanding of the subject.

According to Hammond, Keeney, and Raiffa, "Anchoring...[is when] considering a decision, the mind gives disproportionate weight to the first information it receives. Initial impressions, estimates, or data anchor subsequent thoughts and judgments."[35] There are two ways in which we see an anchoring effect in the models of the Church. First, since everyone prior to the council was presented with the institutional model of the Church, or if they were Protestant, the herald model, these two models have the tendency to anchor any further consideration. A Catholic would have to "get over" the institutional model, much as a Protestant would the herald model, before they could grasp the widening possibilities offered by the developments in ecclesiology. Rather than the mystery of the Church being primary, as Cardinal Dulles asserts in the book, the dominant model remains primary and other insights are added onto it. This anchoring trap narrows the gains offered by Dulles's approach.

A second instance of the anchoring trap can be seen in a very deliberate attempt by some theologians after the Council to take control of the debate by having the "first word." Prior to the documents of the Council getting into wide circulation and certainly before they could be studied and commented upon, Professor Dr. Küng deliberately sought to anchor the reception of the "Spirit of the Council" with his book *The Church*. He was not the only one, but he is the only one to my knowledge to have described his plan to do so in an autobiography:

> I no longer know precisely what day it was in October 1963 (at all events towards the evening I am sitting with the Canadian ecumenist Gregory Baum over a coffee on the Via Vittorio Veneto and putting him in the picture). After perhaps two weeks of brooding and fretting over what evidently cannot be achieved at the Council in the Constitution on the Church it has suddenly dawned on me that I should formulate the new theological synthesis myself. Given the circumstances, it can't be expected from the Council. After the Council, people will be glad of a wider interpretation of the Council constitution—to work on further in the church

and the ecumenical world. In practice this means that instead of wasting my energy in the Theological Commission I should invest it in an ecclesiological synthesis in the spirit of the Council…that same day I sit at my desk in my little hotel room. In perhaps two hours of complete self-forgetfulness I draft for myself a coherent, consistent and transparent conception of the book. It is to have the simple yet demanding title "Essence of the Church" or "The Church."[36]

As is apparent from his own words, Küng sought the first word as a way of anchoring the interpretation of *Lumen Gentium*.

The status-quo trap describes a bias toward the familiar. "Decision makers display, for example, a strong bias toward alternatives which perpetuate the status quo."[37] Research by Hammond, Keeney, and Raiffa has shown that the trap is most significant when individuals or groups are confronted with a decision involving two outcomes. The status quo exerts a distorting effect on the decision.[38]

As can be seen from the "Profession of Faith" of Msgr. Marcel Lefebvre, his heuristic was employed by the Lefeverists in much the same way as Küng employed the anchoring trap.[39] The point here is to illustrate the power and presence of heuristics in Church life, not to engage the revisionist/traditionalist conflict.

While we can identify these first two heuristics in the early days of the implementation of the Council reforms, the next heuristic, the sunk-cost trap, emerges later. The sunk-cost trap is a routine that anchors present-day decisions in the decisions of the past. Hammond, Keeney, and Raiffa write, "Another of our deep-seated biases is to make choices in a way that justifies past choices, even when the past choices no longer seem valid….Our past decisions become what economists call sunk-costs—old investments of time or money that are now irrecoverable."[40] An example of this would be the tremendous efforts expended by American dioceses to implement the reform of the Second Vatican Council on the liturgy. As the reception of the Council by the universal Church began to refine and reshape the implementation, especially after the Extraordinary Synod of 1985, dioceses clung to the original programs because they had invested so much into them that it was impossible for them to envision "starting over."

A contemporary example of this heuristic is the controversy over the retranslation of the texts of the Roman Missal. It refers to the emotional investment in past decisions. In a sense, and this is a generalization, the sunk-cost heuristic is often seen among the progressive members of the Church in the United States.

The confirming-evidence trap is a very subtle psychological process. It refers to how we see evidence. If we have an investment in a specific outcome, we will tend to notice evidence that confirms that outcome and not any other. Hammond, Keeney, and Raiffa express it thus:

> There are two fundamental psychological forces at work here. The first is our tendency to subconsciously decide what we want to do before we figure out why we want to do it. The second is our inclination to be more engaged by things we like than by things we dislike—a tendency well documented even in babies. Naturally, we are drawn to information that supports our subconscious leanings.[41]

Each of us can think of examples of this heuristic. Since I have been attaching groups to each of these routines, I should be fair and say that the confirming-evidence heuristic can be seen in the conservative members of the Church today, who, because they are convinced about a corrective move, tend to argue toward conclusions. In doing so, they exhibit the confirming-evidence heuristic.

Another decision trap is called framing.[42] It is, in some ways, the most important of all heuristics. Hammond, Keeney, and Raiffa tell us,

> The first step in making a decision is to frame the question. It's also one of the most dangerous steps. The way the problem is framed can profoundly influence the choices you make.... The framing trap can take many forms...it is often closely related to other psychological traps. A frame can establish the status quo or introduce an anchor. It can highlight sunk-costs or lead you toward confirming evidence.[43]

There are other heuristics that cognitive science has identified in decision processes, but these examples are sufficient to illustrate the point about how models can close down rather than open up theological understanding. Again, Cardinal Dulles warned his readers about a misuse of his method. He wrote,

> Because images are derived from the finite realities of experience, they are never adequate to represent the mystery of grace. Each model of the Church has its weaknesses; no one should be canonized as the measure of all the rest. Instead of searching for some absolutely best image, it would be advisable to recognize that the manifold images given to us by Scripture and Tradition are mutually complementary. They should be made to interpenetrate and mutually qualify one another. None, therefore, should be interpreted in an exclusivistic sense, so as to negate what the other approved models have to teach us.[44]

The reception of the first edition of *Models of the Church* suffered from many, if not all, of these heuristic traps. While intended by Dulles as a descriptive exploration, which is clear from the above text, readers responded with a proscriptive use of the models, falling at once into the various heuristic traps already identified. It is for this reason that we have spent so much time examining heuristic distortions. This is not to criticize the use of models, which is a very good addition to theological method, but it is to warn us about how models are susceptible to the very psychological processes of distortion that we have seen take place through the misuse of Dulles's work. As noted earlier, this awareness helps us to understand Dulles's decision to return to the modeling project and to offer a corrective.

In 1982, cognizant of this problem of people going through the cafeteria line and choosing what they like (with the attendant distortions in those choices or decisions because of the heuristics), Dulles moved to explore this question in his book *A Church to Believe In*.[45] In 1987, he would revise and expand *Models of the Church* to include a sixth, synthetic model, which is more suited to proscriptive use. Let us now turn our attention to an examination of the sixth model of the Church, the community of disciples.

In constructing his synthetic sixth model of the Church, the community of disciples, Cardinal Dulles begins with the communion model. He does so because this model takes us closest to the opening doctrine of *Lumen Gentium* that the Church is Mystery. From this basis, he then takes insights from the first encyclical of Pope John Paul II, *Redemptor Hominis*. Then he adds developments regarding the idea of *communio* from the Extraordinary Synod of 1985, which articulated the theology of communion as the interpretive key to the entire hermeneutic of Vatican II. His efforts at a synthetic model were seeking integration in the context of the polarization after Vatican II.[46]

Communion defines the purpose of the Church. The Church is not, as Methodist bishop William Willimon has said, sarcastically, "a voluntary association of like-minded individuals gathered together to promote the cause of Jesus."[47] No, the Church exists for communion between the Father and the Son and the Holy Spirit and all the nations of the Earth. This definition preserves the missionary imperative and the basic communitarian structure. What is needed is a way to envision the other four models as organically related to communion.

With integration as a goal, Dulles builds the new model first on a biblical foundation, again using images. He builds the image by studying the degrees of community that can be identified in the New Testament, specifically the following:

1. an outer circle comprising a relatively considerable number of men and women

2. the Twelve

3. Peter, James, and John

4. Peter as rock and shepherd

5. Mary, the Mother of Jesus and chief disciple[48]

The image or model of the disciple is deeply christological. Jesus is the center of the community. Regardless of the degree of community in which we find ourselves, we are disciples of Jesus. There can be no other reference point. The tasks of the disciple are all related to Jesus. We are to sit at his feet, learn from him, hear his words, share his life, constitute a contrast society, share in his redemptive suffering, and become his witnesses even to the ends of the earth.[49]

The life of the disciple is constituted and sustained by the word and sacraments. Preaching and each of the seven sacraments has a discipleship dimension. In this way, Dulles incorporates the insights from the herald and sacramental models of the Church into his synthetic model. The servant model is included as the realization of the life and works of charity that distinguish the disciples as a contrast community.

Dulles maintains his suspicions about the institutional model, which, in the first edition of the book, he claims is the one model that cannot be a basis for synthesis. He strengthens his criticism in the expanded edition when he writes,

> Faith includes, to be sure, a dimension of intellectual ascent, but this element follows a more general commitment to the community and its corporate vision….For this reason, faith cannot be adequately transmitted in the cold atmosphere of the classroom or lecture hall….It is most successfully passed on by trusted masters in a network of interpersonal relationships resembling the community life of Jesus and the Twelve…. Response to the Lord in prayer and worship is essential to any living faith.[50]

As examples of this insight, Dulles then offers the experience in Latin America of the base communities or in North America with the charismatic prayer groups. His point is that the missionary mandate cannot be fulfilled by an institution. It can only be achieved by disciples.

As we consider the missionary mandate, Dulles identifies a key element in the life of the Community of Disciples—its role as a contrast society. He notes,

> In the early centuries, the Church expanded not so much because of concentrated missionary efforts, but through its

power of attraction as a contrast society....Seeing the mutual love and support of Christians and the high moral standard they observed, pagans sought entrance into the Church.... The same is not happening today, largely because the Church is not conspicuous as a community of disciples transformed by its participation in the new creation.[51]

Finally, in my experience of the last ten years of teaching ecclesiology to seminarians and graduate students of theology and ministry, Dulles's synthetic model of the community of disciples offers a vital, needed corrective to the Church in North America today. In the pastor-training program of the Archdiocese of Chicago, I have come to use only this synthetic model as a way for the new pastors to try to overcome the polarization in the local communities they are called to govern.[52] Its synthetic and proscriptive nature makes it a valuable tool in pastoral ministry.

ECUMENISM

In all his work on ecumenical topics, one of the key contributions of Avery Dulles was his method of identification of distinctives. In his extensive career, he always insisted that theology must concern itself with specific propositions, so that distinctive content can be properly understood and studied. This was not a call for a return to the old manualist method, which he studied and appreciated early in his career, but recognized as inadequate for the contemporary task of theology. At the same time, however, he has constantly asserted that content is of the essence of the theological task, and for better or worse, this requires propositions. As already mentioned, his method is especially good for the identification of distinctives and is one of the key contributions he has made to the ecumenical movement.

In the formal, official commissions of the ecumenical movement, especially centered around the Faith and Order Commission of the World Council of Churches, there are three methodological approaches that are sequential. The first is the *comparative ecclesiology* approach. (These methods are named for the projects they were first developed to accomplish.) In this approach, the goal is a clear articulation and understanding of the actual doctrine of the dialogue partner.[53] The second approach, the *Christological method*, seeks to overcome incompatible formulations by a return to the sources and working the question forward into a new proposition that can act as a bridge uniting the seemingly contradictory ones of history.[54] These two methodologies have offered much to the ecumenical movement. Dulles's insistence on the necessity of content and the need to pay attention to distinctiveness have, in a unique way, served those who use the comparative ecclesiology method, which we will discuss further.

In the last decade, the term *new ecumenism* has gained some popularity. I first heard the term from John H. Armstrong and tracked it back to James M. Kushiner, and then to Richard John Neuhaus, and from him to Thomas Oden.[55] Others have attached it to the *Princeton Proposal for Christian Unity*.[56] For our purposes today, we will use James Kushiner's simple definition: "an ecumenism flourishing outside of official ecumenical agencies, generally occurring among traditional Christians, often at the grass roots level."[57] It is an ecumenism of mere Christianity, using *mere* not in the sense of least common denominator, but in the original way that word was defined in the English language, "pure, undiluted, unaltered."[58]

I have often lectured on how ecumenism cannot be approached as diplomatic relations or doctrinal problems solved by bureaucratic processes; rather, ecumenism is about a relationship of trust in which men and women of goodwill, seekers after the truth, study together, pray together, and seek openness to the Holy Spirit, who will alone heal the wounds of division. In fact, we are establishing a contrast society over against the communities of division, a point that we will explore later.

Cardinal Dulles was one of the first and leading Catholics to engage this emerging form of ecumenism through his participation in Evangelicals and Catholics Together (ECT). This important process, chaired by Father Richard John Neuhaus and Charles Colson, has explored the central theological issues that separate Catholics and Protestants since the Reformation. Beginning in 1992, its principal achievements include the first ECT statement: "The Christian Mission in the Third Millennium," issued in 1994.[59] "The Gift of Salvation" was issued in 1997.[60] "Your Word Is Truth" was a sustained study of the Word of God, issued in 2002.[61] "The Communion of Saints" was issued in 2003,[62] and most recently, "The Call to Holiness" in 2005.[63]

Evangelicals and Catholics Together is a theological enterprise. The group has no authority other than their arguments and their witness. Yet, at a time in the ecumenical movement when the formal, official dialogues are at a standstill, it has been singularly significant that the "unlikely bedfellows" of Catholics and Evangelicals can make so much progress unofficially. I personally hold out much hope for these unofficial processes. Evangelicals and Catholics Together is a model that others are following. I have personally participated in two such significant efforts. The first was the *Pro Oriente* Consultation on the Syriac Tradition, which produced six volumes of theological product on the relationships of the churches of the Assyrian and Oriental Orthodox communions.[64] The other facilitated by *ACT3: Accessing the Christian Tradition in the Third Millennium*, has produced two books: *Understanding the Four Views on Baptism* and *Understanding Four Views on the Lord's Supper*.[65] All these efforts have had a widespread effect.

Cardinal Dulles suggested that we need to enter a period of renewed apologetics as a prior step to the kind of theological dialogue envisioned by the comparative ecclesiology method. The reason for this assertion on his part is that those engaged in dialogue frequently are not properly grounded in their own traditions and they cannot manage the demands of the comparative method. Far from being a negative comment toward the ecumenical goal, it is a realistic assessment of the current situation and merely echoes Vatican II's requirement that those who represent a church in ecumenical dialogue be truly competent in their own theology.[66]

CONCLUSION

By describing the finding Cardinal Dulles reports from the use of this method in the first edition of *Models of the Church*, we were able, first, to appreciate how his method expands and deepens our appreciation for the mystery of the Church. Second, we considered some of the pitfalls inherent in the modeling project because of the heuristic effect of models, and how some people in the church used Cardinal Dulles's models proscriptively rather than descriptively. Third, we examined the development of his thought in the revision of the book for its second edition, which addressed this proscriptive use of models through the development of a synthetic sixth model, the community of disciples. Finally, we examined a very small part of Cardinal Dulles's contribution to the ecumenical movement.

Throughout, Avery Cardinal Dulles offered a tremendous service to Christ and his Church through the vocation of theologian. The fact that the symposium out of which this book arises required two keynote addresses and five seminars to examine adequately only the principal areas of his contribution is itself a measure of Dulles's greatness.

1

THEOLOGIAN
OF THE CHURCH

Aidan Nichols, OP

Avery Dulles's first work was a study of the fifteenth-century
Florentine Lay Dominican Giovanni Pico della Mirandola,[1] and so
it is not without some fittingness, or what Thomas Aquinas would have
called *convenientia*, that a Dominican from Europe is speaking about
Cardinal Dulles in his ninetieth year. Indeed, that dissertation, which
won the Harvard essay prize, is an indicator of what was to come, not
only through its brilliance and its thoroughness in the marshaling of
sources, but also, in a way, through its choice of topic and the way it
treated that topic.[2]

The ostensible purpose of Dulles's study is to show the fundamentally Scholastic—rather than Neo-Platonist, Cabbalist, or proto-Idealist—
nature of Pico's thought. We do not have to go far into the book before
a deluge of evidence persuades us that such is the case.[3] The study then
becomes, rather, an exploration of the meaning and truth of the academic title awarded Pico by admiring contemporaries, *princeps concordiae*,
the "prince of concord," a pun on his inherited genealogical title, Conte
di Concordia. My chief, original claim is that, whether consciously or
subconsciously, Cardinal Dulles was profoundly influenced by the title
given to Pico, a title that, after all, Dulles selected for one of his own
books.

In *Princeps Concordiae*, Dulles shows how Pico sought to introduce
a *pax philosophica*—notably between Aristoteleans and Platonists, Thomists
and Scotists. Pico sought so to do without, however, the sacrifice of key

principles by one who, in various intellectual engagements—in his meta-physical realism, for example, and acceptance of the essence/existence distinction—was *au fond* a member of the Thomist household. True, on some occasions, faced with two equally attractive theses, Pico sought, in Dulles's words, "to combine both ideas, although they are mutually exclusive."[4] But overall, for Dulles, the irenicism of Pico della Mirandola served his thought well.

The desire to inaugurate a *pax theologica* by combining the perspectives and insights of a variety of theological approaches and schools is a pervasive feature of Cardinal Dulles's own work. But his is not a facile syncretism, willing to tolerate blatant contradictions and unwilling to identify errors or false evaluations for what they are. In his introduction to *Princeps Concordiae*, seeking to distinguish Pico's humanism from the variety espoused by "modern philosophical idealists," Dulles proposes to show how Pico avoids an "individualist, anthropocentric, and immanent-ist…exaltation of man";[5] that careful avoidance is something that might also be said of Dulles's own interventions in contemporary intra-Catholic debates. Dulles remarks of Pico's cosmology, that he "adopted elements from many traditions without ever succeeding in molding them into a clear-cut-system of his own."[6] While Cardinal Dulles did not give us a systematics in the ecclesiology of *The Catholicity of the Church* (1985)[7] or the theology of faith in the concluding chapters of *The Assurance of Things Hoped For* (1994),[8] we can observe a mind at work that has an impulse toward a more vigorous system than Pico della Mirandola's, this first, if flawed, hero of Dulles's work.

It is not excessive to say that *Princeps Concordiae* already raises, if obliquely, the four Dullesian themes on which we will concentrate: revelation as received by mind and heart, the nature of theology, the role of culture, and the catholicity of Catholicism. These are four themes that, among them, account for the lion's share of Dulles's writing about the faith and life of the Church *ad intra*.

How does this book, published as it was at the astonishingly early age of twenty-two, lead into our (and his) chosen topics? While principally a work of philosophy, of which Dulles's only other book-length exploration is the coauthored *Introductory Metaphysics* (1955),[9] Pico's treatment of philosophy as *inchoatio religionis*, the "beginning of religion," obliged both Pico and Dulles to touch in some way on our quartet of issues.

- First, and most importantly, on *revelation as received by mind and heart*: Dulles notes how for Pico the objects of *faith and reason* "frequently overlap."[10] How to mediate the relations of the two is a preoccupation, even if not the predominant one, of *The Assurance of Things Hoped For.* In this same connection, Dulles remarks on Pico's tendency to place excessive emphasis on "certitude of evidence,"[11] and this phrase may jolt the memories of retentive readers of Dulles's *A History of Apologetics* (1971), as well as of the earlier *Apologetics and the Biblical Christ* (1963).[12] Dulles's preferred approach to apologetics, which reflects, among other things, a lifelong interest in his fellow theologian–cardinal John Henry Newman (witness his 2002 book of that name), is wary of such evidentialist claims to certitude.[13]

- Second, as to the *nature of theology*, with an admiring side reference to the work of Etienne Gilson, Dulles describes how Pico overlooked the way that "in their methods and aims, theology and philosophy are specifically distinct."[14] Dulles's essay collection, *The Craft of Theology* (1992), shows him commending a view of theology where theology emerges, somewhat over against his fellow Jesuit Bernard Lonergan's account, as an intellectual discipline unique in its method, since it is mastered by an eminently unique source, namely, the divine revelation that Dulles studied descriptively in *Revelation Theology: A History* (1971), and more prescriptively in *Models of Revelation* over ten years later.[15]

- Third, the *role of culture* appears in the way the cities and academies of Padua and Florence in Pico's time served, in Dulles's description, as conduits of not only a still vigorous Christian Scholasticism and a newly emerging Renaissance humanism, but also Cabbalistic lore and the remnants of Arab philosophy. Awareness of the cultural *Umwelt* as a factor that the mission of the Church can never ignore is quietly pervasive in a few essays in what may be termed "pastoral ecclesiology" in, for instance, Dulles's *The Resilient Church* (1977) and *The Reshaping of Catholicism* (1988).[16]

• Fourth and finally, as to *catholicity*, Pico's attempt to exhibit Christ as the center of an inspired wisdom found, not just in the divine Scriptures and the Church's Tradition, but in pagan sages meditating on the structure of the cosmos as well, may be linked to Dulles's venture of identifying in Catholicism both a "catholicity from above," deriving directly from the Holy Trinity, and a "catholicity from below," where all the aspirations of nature are fulfilled and superfulfilled in the fullness of divinity that dwells bodily in Christ, a "pleroma" or plenitude in which his Church participates. That is a major theme of his *The Catholicity of the Church* already mentioned, but, judging by his remarks in *Reflections on a Theological Journey*, he regarded a sacramental vision of the Church—such as the aforedescribed perspective opens up—as the best claimant to our ecclesiological allegiance among those canvassed in his most widely diffused book, *Models of the Church* (1974).[17]

All four themes—faith and reason, the nature of theology, the role of culture, and the catholicity of the Church, the latter two of which we will bracket together—are of course aspects of that "fundamental theology" that Avery Dulles practiced as a consummate master.

THE REVEALED FAITH RECEIVED BY MIND AND HEART

Let us now turn to the first and most substantial of the four themes of such fundamental theology. This first motif sets the tone for all life in the Church: the revealed faith received by mind and heart. Apart from (no doubt) obedience to Jesuit superiors, why did Avery Dulles spend so much time on the topic of divine revelation? *Revelation Theology: A History* provides a vantage point. Writing against those who wished to deflate the importance of this theologically vital epistemological topic, Dulles remarks with typical understatement: "While revelation is not the sum and substance of Christianity, it has a certain logical priority in the Christian scheme of things."[18]

He defined *revelation* in refreshingly plain terms: a "free manifestation by God of that which lies beyond the normal reach of human inquiry."[19] If that seems principally focused on the truth of revealed propositions, the wider context of the revelatory divine action is summoned when he adds, "It is the initial action by which God emerges from his hiddenness, calls to man, and invites him to a covenant-existence."[20] Evidence of Dulles's Pico-like desire for a *pax theologica* emerges quickly when we read that revelation "is apprehended as much through significant facts, intuitions of value, and symbolic imagery as through clear and distinct ideas."[21]

In this important formulation, Dulles not only heralds what will be in *Models of Revelation* (1983), his own attempt to make the most of the various models by an account of revelation as "symbolic mediation." He also commits himself here to the view that revelation includes, alongside historical claims, value judgments and symbolic expressiveness, those "clear and distinct ideas." That is a reference to Descartes, and so might strike some as ironic, but Gilson had already shown, rather in the spirit of Dulles's study of Pico, how much the writings of Descartes owe to the patrimony of Christian Scholasticism.[22] To the regret of some of his admirers in the 1980s and 1990s, Dulles never abandoned concern for the propositional element in revelation, an element that provides essential hermeneutical keys for the interpretation of symbolic facts.[23]

Where does Dulles put the accent in terms of the Christian writers of almost two millennia, bearing in mind that it is with the eighteenth-century Enlightenment that the issue of revelation moves center stage? It cannot be said that Dulles evinces much enthusiasm for the theology of revelation found in the modern Scholastics, even such patristic-oriented figures, among them as the nineteenth-century Roman School Jesuits, Giovanni Perrone and Johann Baptist Franzelin. Where he singles out a Thomist for praise, it is the Cologne theologian Matthias Joseph Scheeben for his emphasis on theological mystery; with Scheeben, he brackets the highly un-Scholastic figure of Newman on this very ground.[24]

Though in *The Assurance of Things Hoped For*, the Baroque Scholastics are quarried for useful material,[25] a cameo of Newman's theology of faith in *Revelation Theology* and elsewhere enables Dulles to sharpen an anti-Scholastic—or perhaps it is only an antirationalist—knife. He cites approvingly the twelfth of Newman's University Sermons, where Newman treats faith as an intellectual act, albeit one "done in a certain moral disposition," but understands this act of the intelligence as "reasonable" only in a very restricted sense. First, it is a "reasoning *upon presumptions*,"[26] and second, the discriminating principle that keeps it from credulity or superstition is not so much reason as it is love. Dulles compares unfavorably with this sermon from Newman's Anglican period the twelve theses on faith he composed at Rome in 1847 in an effort to present his thought in a more classically Latin-Catholic fashion.[27] The formulations exacted by the same curial theologians from Newman's French contemporary, the Abbé Louis Bautain, contain, Dulles judges, "some theologically unfortunate expressions."[28] This cryptic phrase undoubtedly refers to the demand for the "certainty of evidence," which, in *Princeps Concordiae*, Dulles had lamented in Pico della Mirandola. He is preparing us for his espousal of the theology of the "eyes of faith" found in the writings of the early twentieth-century French Jesuit Pierre Rousselot, who fell in the First World War. Along with the commitment to Newman, the devotion to Rousselot is crucial in Cardinal Dulles's approach to the issue of revelation received by mind and heart.

Rousselot's account of faith is found in a celebrated two-part essay, "Les Yeux de la foi," which appeared in the Strasbourg *Revue des Sciences Religieuses* (1910), and in English translation, in book form, under the title *The Eyes of Faith and Answer to Two Attacks* (1991). Cardinal Dulles collaborated on this project with his confrere, Father John McDermott, a Rousselot specialist.[29] Concerned that the signs of credibility (miracle, the fulfillment of prophecy) were treated by more conventional Scholastics as essentially extraneous to the revelation to which they testified, Rousselot insisted that the revelation was itself the significance of the signs that were, therefore, not extraneous to its content but intrinsically related thereto. The signs of credibility are guides, not only to the historical actuality of the fact of revelation, but also to the meaning of its content. As Dulles remarked in his contribution to the Rousselot translation, "scientific history" is not "capable of settling the question of religious interpretation," for the simple reason that "such interpretation lies within the competence of a man committed, or at least open, to religious values."[30]

In his *Apologetics and the Biblical Christ*, Dulles had exemplified Rousselot's approach by seeking a "confessional apologetic," which would "exhibit concurrently the credibility of the essential facts and of their Christian interpretation. It would invite the inquirer to assent to both in one indivisible act."[31] Cardinal Dulles wished us not to concentrate on micromanaging the evidence of Christ's divine legateship in prophecy and miracle, though he had written movingly about both in the narrative of his conversion, *A Testimonial to Grace* (1946).[32] While there may be in this shift of perspective an element of *proskunesis* before the gods of exegetical fashion, he also wanted us, more positively, to take the widest possible view of credibility along the lines of a long-forgotten work he greatly admired, Jean Levie's *Sous les Yeux de l'incroyant*, for which the great argument that renders faith credible is "the whole Christ in His Church."[33] From scanning the overall Christian landscape, a configuration of meaning emerges that both tallies and impresses because it makes sense of so much in human experience, while also wonderfully surpassing it. As Maurice Blondel, another hero of Dulles's *oeuvre*, would have it, revelation offers our natural being fulfillment even as it simultaneously offers it superfulfillment.[34]

This explains why, aside from Newman and Rousselot, Dulles's nineteenth-century enthusiasms are reserved for the Catholic Tübingen school, notably Johann Sebastian von Drey, who saw revelation as God's self-revelation through historical acts climaxing in the incarnation, and the Church as its organic continuation. But the mark of Franzelin, not Drey, lies on the Dogmatic Constitution *Dei Filius* of the First Vatican Council. Consonantly, while Dulles praises that text for its "conceptual clarity," he also laments its lack of "biblical and existential tone," for which we must seek elsewhere.[35]

Eschewing the Catholic Modernists,[36] Dulles looked to twentieth-century theology for a more "serene" discussion of the exegetical, historical, and philosophical difficulties the Modernists raised.[37] This is where *la nouvelle théologie* scores. Blondel, lionized by the *nouvelle théologie*, spent much of his life under a cloud, which in Pius XII's encyclical *Humani Generis* (1950), looked as though it might turn to rain, but Dulles regards the encyclical as merely a benign warning against underrating the gains of Scholasticism in terms of exact conceptual thought.[38] Certainly, the more biblical and existential tone Dulles desired was better represented in *Dei Verbum*, the Dogmatic Constitution on Divine Revelation of the Second Vatican Council, to which Henri de Lubac's christocentric concept of revelation—another version of Levie's "the whole Christ in His Church"—was a vital contributor.

Dulles signals his acceptance of de Lubac's approach when he selects, as the supreme summary of the difference the New Testament makes, the opening words of the Letter to the Hebrews with their contrast between divine communication in the Old Testament *polymerôs kai polytropôs*, "in many and various ways," with a new and definitive speaking *en huiô*, "by a Son" (Heb 1:1–2).[39] Recapitulating the theology of another John, the Beloved Disciple, "revelation...does not really differ from the gift of eternal life in the Son."[40] That gives revelation not only an absolutely clear historical rooting but also a future-oriented, eschatological character. As Dulles points out, for the Johannine letters, the life announced by the apostolic witnesses "will not be seen as it truly is until he appears at the end."[41] Dulles was tempted by the notion of the Incarnate Word Christ as subsistent revelation, which he accepted with the qualifiers that this is so inasmuch as "his inner secret becomes manifest through his words and deeds, and through the communication of his Spirit to those who believe."[42]

In an immediately postconciliar perspective, Dulles's survey, in *Revelation Theology*, of younger theologians in the North America of the later 1960s, anticonceptualist and pragmatist to a man, was already sending a signal about the possible failure of the *pax theologica* he sought. Dulles warns against theology in the new world ceasing to learn from the voices of Europe—he means, surely, the voices of Western Europe's *nouvelle théologie*, among whom the preconciliar Edward Schillebeeckx and Karl Rahner were still at this date counted—and he ends with an admonition to Catholic theologians to attain greater unanimity about the meaning of truth, failing which the Modernist crisis will remain always with us.

Dulles used the conclusion of his survey of revelation theology to present an early anticipation of the taxonomic approach that will issue not just a few years later in *Models of the Church*, but also, a decade passing, in *Models of Revelation*. The spirit of the *pax theologica* falls on him once more when he declares that each of three mentalities or models—factual, conceptual, and mystical—has its place: "Revelation is never mere fact, in the sense of a verifiable historical occurrence; it is a fact pregnant with an abiding divine significance. Revelation is never mere doctrine, in the sense of abstract propositional truth; it is always doctrine which illumines a unique event."[43]

THE NATURE OF THEOLOGY

The Craft of Theology provides an obvious way into the next topic, the nature of theology. The introduction gives a neat statement of his view of the Church as he saw it at the beginning of the 1990s. While accepting that magisterial interventions in the theological articulation of doctrine might sometimes be inopportune, he also regarded them as not infrequently "necessary to prevent the erosion of the faith."[44] It is a topic he would return to both in this "manifesto" and, at greater length, in *Magisterium: Teacher and Guardian of the Faith* (2007).[45] But more importantly for our subject, and more intrinsically desirable, if not necessarily more efficacious, was what he called the capacity of theology to "discipline itself by consensus-forming procedures." The "excessive uniformity" of immediately preconciliar theology might explain, but it could not justify, the inability of postconciliar theologians to recognize necessary parameters of theological inquiry or the desirability of coherence in the overall theological culture of the Church. Today, "theologians lack a common language, common goals, and common norms." Consequently, *odium theologicum* had reached a level of intensity rarely attained except in schismatic or potentially schismatic situations. While Dulles expresses himself less apocalyptically, we have not inflated his meaning, not least because his own prescription to the patient is a clearer recognition of the "ecclesial character" of theology. Offering that medicine would not make sense unless the sickness diagnosed was the tendentially schismatic or sectarian character of much theological life. Dulles himself puts it in terms of a loss of identity of much Catholic theology, but he adds that this disappearing identity follows from ceasing to "be a reflection on the faith of the Church."[46] This bears out my interpretation of his remarks, even though legitimate problems sometimes arise as to how that faith is itself to be determined. An autobiographical context was furnished by his *Reflections on a Theological Journey* (1996), published within the same covers as a reprinting of *A Testimonial to Grace*.[47] This memoir bears witness to a certain weariness with the making of *pax theologica*: peace fatigue.[48]

Situating himself against the backdrop of predecessors and contemporaries, Dulles was willing to identify himself, up to a point, as a "post-critical" theologian. Critical scholarship and theology, from the mid-eighteenth century on, were insufficiently critical of their own critiques. Taken neat, like malt whisky, the stance of criticism subverts all voluntary engagements. When, as now, cognitive skepticism about morals and faith tends to rule, it is more important to show how firm epistemic commitments in these areas may still be responsible human acts. In any case, any starting point from which critical doubt is exercised depends on a network of beliefs, which themselves might be doubted should one choose. As he puts it, all criticism "rests on a fiduciary basis."[49] Moreover, hypercriticism is often hypocrisy, since its program applies selectively with a view to destroying a limited number of beliefs, notably those touching revealed religion. Its proponents conveniently forget that no one can forward an intellectual project without relying on the authority of others whose testing of evidence is accepted; in this way, knowledge has an inescapable "social dimension."[50] Knowledge also has what Dulles terms, in dependence on the Hungarian philosopher Michael Polanyi, a "tacit dimension." This may be tacitness of presuppositions again, but it may also be the tacit understanding of clues that point the way to a conclusion without being able to yield a formal argument—a feature of Dullesian apologetics.[51]

Positively, Dulles sets out three claims for the unique modus operandi of theology, all of which turn on its relation to the act of faith, or the life of faith. First, theology has an epistemics of participation: "The contents of faith are known not by merely detached observation but by indwelling or participation, somewhat as we know our own body with its powers and weaknesses."[52] Second, theology's contents are aspects of a total, not-fully-objectifiable vision of reality. A computer might be able to derive conclusions from dogmatic statements considered simply as propositions, but this is not the same thing. Third, theology is reliant on the community of the Church, which is the primary bearer of faith. A theologian who "seeks to work without the support of fellow believers has forfeited a necessary resource for the theological enterprise."[53]

All of that is summed up by saying that the proper method of theology depends on a "connoisseurship derived from personal appropriation of the living faith of the Church."[54]

The word *connoisseurship* might be replaced, perhaps, by *tact* or *empathy* or *connaturality*—in fact, Dulles does use *connaturality* as an occasional synonym[55]—but its associations with the evaluation of art make it especially appropriate to Dulles's project. Much of theology consisted for him in the "correct articulation of the Christian symbols," a reference to the imaginative texture of the way revelation is given in its accredited witnesses, Scripture and Tradition. Since the thirteenth century, we have been accustomed to regard theology as primarily a science. But for Dulles, it was chiefly an "art," and moreover, congruently with what has just been said about theology's unique mode of working, an "art acquired through familiarity with being at home in the community in which the symbols function."[56] One must rely on the symbols as cues, and Dulles illustrates this by invoking the liturgy. As he writes, "Liturgy has regularly been recognized as a prime theological source and it is securely established in this role by postcritical theology."[57] Theology must retain close bonds with prayer and worship, or it will, in his words, "regress." Theological speculation about God must take account not only of the demands of conceptual reasoning but also of the requirements of worship.

Connoisseurship ought to enable one to judge what is or is not consonant with revelation. Molded in part, no doubt, by the liturgy, the sense of the faithful is such connoisseurship in its primordial form, which theology refines. Both the liturgy and the sense of the faithful belong to Tradition, as one of the two mandated sources of theology, and Dulles was inclined to share Blondel's account of Tradition as no mere surrogate for the lack of exhaustive written records, but rather a living reality that is future oriented—indeed, eschatologically oriented. Dulles cites approvingly Blondel's description of Tradition in *History and Dogma* as "the guardian of the initial gift insofar as it has not yet been formulated nor even expressly understood."[58] Tradition, like Scripture in its imagistic aspect, is an example, as Dulles says, of "tacit knowledge,"[59] but it is also a unique example of such knowledge in that it is not only "pneumatological," given by the Spirit, but "eschatological," an orientation to the complete unveiling of all that is granted in the apostolic revelation, in the vision of God and of all things in God at the end of the age.

CULTURE AND THE CATHOLICITY OF THE CHURCH

Meanwhile, we must live in the Church catholic throughout in-between times, and thus, in culture, which is the soil where distinctively human things grow. As Dulles himself informs us, his discovery of the approach of models was indebted to H. Richard Niebuhr, and notably to Niebuhr's taxonomy of theological attitudes to culture in his *Christ and Culture*, written at the beginning of the 1950s.[60] But Dulles was concerned not only with Niebuhr's method, which could be applied in other domains, as Dulles indeed did; he was also interested in Niebuhr's subject matter.

That subject matter was vital to a Church that, at the Second Vatican Council, had acknowledged more fully than before the importance of the cultural domain as a framework, or even an intermediary, in the relation of God and souls.[61] It was an acknowledgment that would be taken further in the pontificate of John Paul II, notably in his establishing the Pontifical Council for Culture, from which founding act there emerged a host of miniature Catholic institutes for faith and culture worldwide.

Dulles rapidly reduced Niebuhr's five types or models to three, and then the three to one. Niebuhr had described five types of relation, which he summed up as the following: Christ against Culture, the Christ of Culture, Christ above Culture, Christ and Culture in Paradox, and Christ the Transformer of Culture. As well as replacing Niebuhr's taxonomic term "types" with his own, "models," Dulles, without much loss of matter, reduces Niebuhr's five categories to three, which are confrontation, synthesis, and transformation. The confrontation model assumes the noncompatibility with cultural expression of the Word of God, which, in its ever-new happening, always stands over against any given configuration of the human. For Dulles, Karl Barth is its representative. For the synthesis model, a specific line of cultural development is providentially prepared (as with ancient Greece and Rome) and put in place as a Christian civilization where faith and culture have uniquely blended to be an irreplaceable patrimony for the future. Thus, the cultural Christendom that spans the Mediterranean basin of the Fathers, continues in the medieval Christendom of Europe, and in early modernity is carried by discovery, colonialization, and mission to much of the rest of the world. For Dulles, Hilaire Belloc is the representative of this. The transformation model, for which Dulles opted, "strikes a kind of balance between the two,"[62] and, as so often, such a balance was for Dulles highly attractive: it is, we might say, the spirit of *pax theologica* even when deprived of its form. He explains, "With the confrontation model, [the transformation model] asserts that Christianity imposes demands on every cultural heritage, calling for continual renewal and reform. With the synthesis model, it holds that Christianity must embody itself in appropriate cultural forms."[63] The religion of the Gospel seeks to transform all the cultures it enters yet itself has features of a culture in that it is "a system of meanings, historically transmitted, embodied in symbols, and instilled into new members of the group so that they are inclined to think, judge, and act in characteristic ways."[64] Such bipolarity matches well the cognate thinking on this topic of Joseph Ratzinger, who later became Pope Benedict XVI.[65] Not only must the Church transform discrete cultures into new shapes; she must also socialize their members into her own overall culture as the universal Church.

In Dulles's preferred version of transformationism, which he calls the "reciprocity theory," while the gospel indeed inserts new objective content into cultures, rather than simply transforming their inner impulse, the cultures that result—like the cultures that exist before or without the gospel—are not hermetically sealed units but are themselves permeable one to another, and able to engage in dialogue one with the other.[66] It is precisely by virtue of such reciprocity that "multiple inculturations" of the faith may be beneficial to the universal Church—and not simply to the inhabitants of each Christianized culture singly taken.[67] As Dulles sagaciously underlines, a contrasting transformationism of autonomy (rather than reciprocity) will tend to produce a federation of regional groups of specific churches, rather than a genuine communion of churches within the one universal Church. Only a transformationism of reciprocity, such as his own, can guarantee a different outcome.

Even belonging to this kind of transformed (local or regional) culture, which has accepted reciprocal relations with others like itself, does not, however, suffice. For the unity of the worldwide Church to have its full impact, one must also be "socialized into the universal church, with its shared meanings, common symbols, and normative behavior patterns."[68] Only a Church with "strong sacramental and hierarchical" features can likely retain a unity across cultures; and he warns against any tendency to "fragment into small, egalitarian base communities."[69]

The key neuralgic point is the issue of *historical concreteness*: "Advocates of cultural autonomy object, not without reason, that the traditional symbols and structures of unity, such as the Bible, creeds, sacraments, episcopacy, and papacy, are shot through with the particularities of Semitic and Western culture and are therefore alienating to non-Westerners."[70] But Dulles insists that this cannot be helped. Concretely, the foundations have been laid in history. Authenticity requires continuity with them. A revelation mediated by the sages and statesmen of Greece and Rome might seem more fitting, but God chose instead as his vehicle a "militaristic, patriarchal, ethnocentric society," namely, Israel.[71] He chose what was weak and foolish even in the cultural order, and the wellsprings of our faith are there. These are the foundations; and while they can be built on and thus extended beyond themselves, they can never be left behind. In the urgent tone that sometimes interrupted his manner of mild reasonableness, Dulles concludes,

> For the sake of the emerging world church, we must resist the conventional view that particularity is divisive, and that inclusiveness must be abstract. To escape the dilemma between

34

segregated concreteness and featureless generality, we must learn to appreciate concrete universality and inclusive particularity. Only in this way will it be possible for the church of the future, with all its cultural differences, to affirm its own origins and its own past history, culturally conditioned though both of these may have been.[72]

Avery Dulles's vision of Church catholic, as of theology, favors contrasts, but is allergic to contradictions. His *pax theologica* would warrant the fulminations of a prophet Jeremiah against those who cry, "'Peace, peace,' when there is no peace" (Jer 6:14), if it sought to say of the holders of theological opinions, with the Dodo in *Alice's Adventures in Wonderland*, "*Everybody* has won and *all* must have prizes."[73] In the words of one of Dulles's favorite Tübingen School authors, Johann Adam Möhler of *Die Einheit der Kirche*, the choirmaster's aim for his singers is harmony not discord. His peace can embrace the counterpoint of *Gegensatz*, but not the unresolvable dissonance of *Widerspruch*. Significantly, that Möhler text is cited on a trio of widely disparate occasions situated at crucial points in Dulles's *The Catholicity of the Church*.[74]

CONCLUSION

As we have seen, for Avery Cardinal Dulles, theology was an artistic "craft." This is an apt word, which, hopefully, was chosen with care. Until the mid-nineteenth-century revival in England of the craftsman-designer with Pugin, Morris, and Burne-Jones, and the subsequent appeal of Maritain for a recovery of the sense of art as reason-engaged-in-making-things, which so influenced Eric Gill and David Jones, craftsmen were at something of a discount. They were not impresarios of the transcendentals, as were pure artists or virtuoso musicians. The kind of reasonable making with which we associate Cardinal Dulles is the craft of the mosaicist. Each piece of mosaic must be carefully cut and chiseled to fit with others in a scheme that is eloquent of meaning and harmoniously ordered. Each piece must also be angled to catch the light. The meticulously selected citations from and references to a massive range of authors, and, more importantly, the arguments these illustrate, are the materials with which Dulles exercised his craft, and they were put together with a skill that gives the impression of consummate ease. The pieces are set in the wall. We stand back, and in the atmosphere of that sweet reasonableness that is the dominant literary ethos of this author, we breathe out the words, "Of course!"

However, the fitting in of the pieces of mosaic one with another to produce an overall scheme that is eloquent of some meaning is not all there is to the art of the mosaicist. There is also the angling to give light. This is not simply the intellectual light of a heuristic process leading to a new discovery through some cognitively fruitful theological thesis, though certainly Cardinal Dulles prized that. It is also a ray of that light that never was on land or sea, the light that is the true illumination of all theology, innovative or otherwise, since it accounts for both the light of faith and the light of glory. It is the uncreated Light, and it shone forth from the Father in the Face of Jesus Christ thanks to the communication of the Holy Spirit.

2

ENGAGING THE WORLD

Paul McPartlan

What is the Church supposed to be doing? One of the threads uniting the work of Cardinal Avery Dulles over five decades has been his desire to give a clear and authentic answer to that question. Dulles received his doctorate in theology in 1960 from the Gregorian University and began teaching at Woodstock as the Second Vatican Council was about to take place—an exciting time to be starting out as a theologian! War and a lengthy Jesuit formation meant that he was already in his forties, but a long and fruitful career lay ahead. In hindsight, we can now see how that career was powerfully shaped by the Council. Immediately following the Council in 1967, he addressed this question: What is the Church supposed to be doing? in his book, *The Dimensions of the Church*, and found the best answer in the Council's Pastoral Constitution on the Church in the Modern World, *Gaudium et Spes*. The Council taught that "whether it aids the world or whether it benefits from it, the Church has but one sole purpose—that the kingdom of God may come and the salvation of the human race may be accomplished."[1] There in a nutshell is what the Church is supposed to be doing.[2]

That text has been a light for Avery Dulles amid all the competing theological and ecclesiological agendas of the postconciliar period, and his own clearheaded accounts of what the Council taught have been a light for many others. Having taught a graduate course on Vatican II for several years, I have often found students to be fascinated and delighted when, after years of having an impression of what the Council taught, they read the documents for themselves. In his 1988 book, *The Reshaping of Catholicism*, Dulles prefaced a skilfull overview of the Council's teaching on the purpose and finality of the Church by summarizing the many variant readings of that teaching. "Without attempting to pass judgement on these various reactions," he said, "I would like to go back to the council documents and try to reconstruct, as objectively as possible, what they actually do say about the purpose of the Church. The experience, I have found, is something like that of a scholar scraping away the surface layer of a palimpsest and discovering, as it were for the first time, the original text beneath it."[3] His analysis brought him back to that text of *Gaudium et Spes*: "The Church has but one sole purpose—that the kingdom of God may come and the salvation of the human race may be accomplished" (GS 45).[4]

Certainly, he added, "the church…does not achieve the salvation of the human race or the completion of the kingdom of God by its own unaided forces. It depends continuously on God, in whose hands it serves as an instrument [LG 9]."[5] Hence, the Council's teaching that the Church is itself a great *sacrament*, "a sign and instrument…of communion with God and of unity among all men" (LG 1), something "at once manifesting and actualizing the mystery of God's love" (GS 45). A decade earlier, in his book *The Resilient Church*, Dulles commented, "According to Vatican II the Church is 'the universal sacrament of salvation' (LG 48). After some years work in ecclesiology, I am inclined to think that there is no better definition." He goes on to state,

> The Church as sacrament must signify and embody the presence of God's saving love in Christ, renewing the face of the earth. We may never take it for granted that the Church is already fully Church. In every generation it must labor to make the redemptive love of Christ, directed toward the whole human family, a tangible and palpable reality. It must draw men and women of every kind and condition into a dynamic union dominated by faith, hope, and charity.[6]

Those are the words of someone with a broad and vigorous understanding of the Church's purpose in a world loved by God and saved by Jesus Christ. This is a Church with a great task to perform in view of humanity at large, a Church with a strong mission *ad extra*. My purpose, here, is to consider how Avery Dulles understood that mission *ad extra*, how he understood the Church as *engaging the world*.

At the beginning of *The Resilient Church*, Dulles states, "There are some events in church history so decisive that they set the agenda for an entire historical era."[7] He was aware, twelve years after its end, that the reverberations of the Council were going to be felt for many years. With that in mind, we will consider Dulles's work in terms of three broad periods: the years of the Council and the early postconciliar period; the middle years, roughly centering on the Extraordinary Synod of 1985, which examined the implementation of the Council twenty years on; and finally, the more recent period, roughly centering on the Jubilee Year 2000, when again the Church's reception of the Council was assessed.

First, however, it is worth pausing to consider *The Resilient Church*'s intriguing title. The author explained that it indicated his conviction "that the Church has the power not simply to accommodate itself to the pressures placed upon it but to respond creatively and to assert counterpressures upon its environment."[8] I am reminded of the telling words that Augustine, as yet unbaptized, heard the Lord say to him: "You will not change me into you, but you will be changed into me."[9] Dulles likewise imagined the Church not simply changing to suit the world, but rather, in and through its always necessary adaptations, challenging the world itself to be changed. He continued: "Unlike many ecclesiastical conservatives, I hold that adaptation need not be a form of capitulation to the world, but that an adapting Church should be able to herald the Christian message with greater power and impact." Nevertheless, he added, "Unlike certain liberals, I am deeply concerned that the Church, in its efforts at adaptation, should avoid imitating the fashions of the non-believing world and should have the courage to be different. Difference is not to be cultivated for its own sake, but it is to be fearlessly accepted when Christ and the gospel so require." Consequently, he said there was a "twofold critique" running through the book, and his own aim was "to combine as far as possible, the daring of the liberal with the caution of the conservative, the openness of the liberal with the fidelity of the conservative."[10] It is the balance, objectivity, and impartiality of Avery Dulles's scholarly work that have gained him so many admirers over the years. He was a free spirit, but a faithful one. It was surely significant that he placed Saint Paul's words to the Corinthians at the start of the book: "I have become all things to all men, that I might by all means save some. I do it for the sake of the gospel, that I might share in its blessings" (1 Cor 9:20–23).[11]

THE EARLY YEARS

In March 1962, Pope John XXIII asked Cardinal Suenens of Malines-Brussels how preparations for the new Council were going, and more specifically, who was looking after an overall plan for the Council. Cardinal Suenens frankly told him that nobody was, and that things were in total disarray.[12] There were, in fact, seventy-two disparate draft documents, with no unity or coherence. Joseph Ratzinger, a young theologian at the time, said that the diligence of the preparatory commissions was "somewhat distressing."[13] Suenens reports that the pope then asked him "to clear the ground and submit to him a plan based on the prepared schemata."[14] He did so in April 1962. The pope had copies of the plan circulated to a few influential cardinals in May, but he did not want to impose it on the Council—he kept it in reserve.

On December 4, 1962, after weeks of mounting unease among the assembled bishops at the lack of an overall program for the Council, Cardinal Suenens finally presented the plan that had been requested and endorsed by Pope John. Significantly, Cardinal Montini, the future Pope Paul VI, had written to the papal Secretary of State on October 18, expressing serious concern over the lack of an organic program and favorably mentioning Suenens's plan.[15] What was the plan? In a preliminary note of March 1962, Suenens proposed grouping all the documents under two headings: first, those dealing with the Church *ad extra*, that is, "the Church as it faces the world of today," and second, those dealing with the Church *ad intra*, that is, "the Church in itself, but with the aim of helping it better to respond to its mission in the world."[16] So, the first group dealt with the Church looking outward to the world, and even the Church's internal affairs dealt with by the second group were to be treated with a view to helping it in its *mission*. The final version of the plan submitted to the pope suggested that "the central question for the whole Council" could be this: "How is the Church of the twentieth century measuring up to the Master's last command: 'Go, therefore, make disciples of all the nations. Baptize them in the name of the Father and of the Son and of the Holy Spirit, and teach them to observe all the commands I gave you'?"[17]

That Gospel text was central to Suenens's speech to the Council on December 4 as he proposed that the Council should be a Council *de Ecclesia*, and that there should be two parts to its work: on the Church *ad intra* and *ad extra*, respectively.[18] In fact, to Suenens's surprise, Pope John had already aired these ideas in his radio broadcast on September 11, 1962, a month before the Council opened. He quoted the Savior's final words in Matthew's Gospel and said that they called for the Church to have vitality both *ad intra* and *ad extra*. The Church had responsibilities to teach and sanctify its own sons and daughters, and to respond to the needs of the world. "The world needs Christ," he said, "and it is the Church which must take Christ to the world."[19] This having been publicly broadcast, Suenens was able to refer to it in his speech, and to say that the program he was proposing was simply an explication of what the Holy Father himself had said. A veil was thereby drawn over where the Holy Father himself had got it from. The bishops applauded and had to be reminded that they weren't supposed to do that.[20]

So, the Council endorsed the plan and the Coordinating Commission duly met in January 1963 to revise the conciliar program. Under the single overall title of *Ecclesia Christi, lumen gentium*,[21] it listed seventeen planned documents, Schema 17 being the first appearance of a proposed document devoted to "The Presence of the Church in the World of Today,"[22] the future *Gaudium et Spes*.[23] With the backing of Pope John, Suenens had delivered a call to action, focusing the Council on the Church's mission in the world. Pope Paul VI, who succeeded Pope John in June 1963, shared the same vision, as we have seen.

In fact, Dulles later quoted Pope Paul's statement that the objectives of Vatican II could all be summed up in one, namely, "to make the Church of the twentieth century even better fitted for proclaiming the Gospel to the people of the twentieth century."[24] The new pope's desire that the Church should engage the world after the pattern of its founder was particularly evident in his first encyclical letter, *Ecclesiam Suam*, issued on

August 6, 1964, the Feast of the Transfiguration, the same feast day on which Paul VI died in 1978. The encyclical proposed *dialogue* with the entire world, understood in terms of three concentric circles around the Catholic Church: the first circle, farthest out, was the entire human race; moving inward, the second circle consisted of all those who worship the one God, especially Jews and Muslims; and the third circle, nearest to hand, consisted of all Christians.[25]

Acknowledging both Suenens's speech and Pope Paul's circles of dialogue, Dulles constructed his book *The Dimensions of the Church* to treat the "outer realms, to which the Church must dynamically relate," namely, "the other Christian communities, the peoples still to be evangelized, and the world of secular life."[26] But those three chapters followed a remarkable first chapter, which gave the book its name, and where Dulles showed how, especially in *Lumen Gentium*, Vatican II had significantly deepened Catholic reflection on the Church and its dimensions, beyond the very institutional vision that had held sway since the time of Bellarmine, who had proposed a strict unity in "creed, code, and cult."[27]

Dulles took Saint Paul's prayer that the Ephesians might comprehend the breadth and length and height and depth of the love of Christ (see Eph 3:18), and analogously considered four newly appreciated aspects of the Church: first, its height, the Church is a heavenly mystery and not just an earthly community; its depth, the Church is also a Church of sinners in need of repentance; its breadth, its mysterious extension outward into the three circles described by Pope Paul; and finally, its length, by which he meant its historical story, originating in the Old Testament, and even before the ages, and extending forward to the communion of saints in the kingdom of heaven, whose life we already anticipate in the liturgy.[28]

Focusing here on the *breadth*, we can surely hear echoes of his Jesuit confrere, Henri de Lubac, and also of the great Dominican Yves Congar when Dulles says, "Most Catholics fail to live up to their name because their own idea of the Church is too small, too narrow, too exclusive."[29] In his book *Catholicism*, de Lubac mapped out a stunning vision: the Catholic Church is "neither Latin nor Greek," he said, "but universal":

In her man's desires and God's have their meeting-place, and
by teaching all men their obligations she wishes at the same
time to satisfy and more than satisfy the yearnings of each soul
and of every age; to gather in everything for its salvation and
sanctification....It is therefore the very opposite of a 'closed
society.'[30]

Dulles stated firmly that "the Church is by nature an open society,"[31] and
he was theologically adventurous as he pondered how its extension
might work, particularly regarding other world religions in the middle
circle. Christ, the incarnate Word, "crowns all the religions of the world,"
he said. "The doctrinal and cultic life which characterizes these other
religions is an adumbration and even an incipient presence of the Church
of Christ."[32]

Regarding the outer circle of secular society, Dulles stressed that
the Church recognized "the intrinsic goodness of the natural order" and
therefore the proper "autonomy of the arts and sciences,"[33] and regarding
the inner circle of other Christians, he welcomed the Council's refusal to
identify the Church of Christ exclusively with Roman Catholicism.
Some, even very many, of the elements of the Church also exist outside
the visible boundaries of the Catholic Church (see *LG* 8),[34] so there are
degrees of being Church, and degrees of communion. It is a sliding scale—
not all or nothing.[35] Five years later, in his lengthy article on "The Church,
the Churches, and the Catholic Church," Dulles noted the important shift
in *Lumen Gentium* 8, from saying exclusively that the Church of Christ *is*
the Catholic Church,[36] to saying that it *subsists in* the Catholic Church—a
change primarily prompted by the desire to recognize elements of the
Church outside the visible boundaries of the Catholic Church.[37] This
implies, he said, that "Vatican II looks upon the Church of Christ as transcending Roman Catholicism."[38] He concluded,

Catholicism is not insuperably opposed to either Orthodox
or Protestant Christianity. Roman Catholicism may prove
capable of enriching these other Christian streams as well as
of profiting from what they have to offer. The more the
Roman Catholic Church is able to participate in this mutual

exchange of riches, the more it may be expected to progress, in fellowship with other Christians, to the fullness Christ wills for His Church.[39]

More than twenty years later, Pope John Paul II would likewise speak of ecumenical dialogue as "an exchange of gifts."[40]

THE MIDDLE YEARS

In 1977, as we move into the middle years, we note that, in *The Resilient Church*, Dulles again highlights the "two foci" of the Council, following Suenens, namely, "the inner renewal of the Roman Catholic Church and the fostering of a more positive and fruitful relationship between the Church and other human communities," and he heeded Suenens's own intuition of the interconnection of these two endeavors: it was expected, he said, "that a more receptive attitude toward external groups and agencies would greatly assist the Catholic Church in its own self-renewal, and that that renewal, in turn, would enable the Church to relate itself more effectively to the rest of the human family." Still following Paul VI's idea of concentric circles, he spoke of the external communities as falling into three groups: "the other Christian churches, the other religions, and the secular culture of our age."[41]

He was concerned, however, that mission seemed to be faltering somewhat in the postconciliar Church, and he set out to investigate why. In an important chapter on "Rethinking the Mission of the Church," he revisited his famous five models of the Church, coined just three years earlier, namely, Church as institution, mystical communion, sacrament, herald, and servant.[42] Mission should not be linked too closely just with the institutional model, he said. In fact, the idea of mission was being enriched by perspectives from the other models, but it was also in danger of being diverted from its true course, especially into an agenda for social reform. Of course, the Church must be concerned to promote social justice, but its "first and foremost task," he insisted, was "to call people to a new life in God—a life mediated especially by faith and worship," and he quoted Paul VI's celebrated text in *Evangelii Nuntiandi* (1975):

"Evangelizing is in fact the grace and vocation proper to the Church, her deepest identity."[43]

In 1975, a rather unique opportunity presented itself for Dulles to clarify these distinctions. He gave evidence to the bicentennial justice hearing, and he spoke on "Dilemmas Facing the Church in the World" as it pursues its social ministry. It would be wrong, he said, to suggest that "the church has no business mixing into socio-political questions,"[44] yet it must be careful as it does so. If it speaks in generalities, it may seem to be timid; if it gets too specific, it can seem to be venturing outside its proper competence. Certainly, the Church must "keep alive the gospel ideals as a norm for social and political life," but it must realize also that few people come to it or remain in it simply because of its social ministry. "They know that the world and its problems will be with them until they die, but they are desperate for a vivifying contact with the eternal Spirit in whom all things begin and end, the God who can bring life even to the dead."[45] What people want most of all is "communion with God," and that most of all is what the Church offers "as the sacrament of Christ in the world of today."[46] This is what he meant when he said in *The Resilient Church* that, as he saw it, the Church's mission was simply "to become the Church…an efficacious sign of Christ."[47]

Clearly, at that time at least, his own favored model was of the Church as sacrament, which he regarded as having exceptional capacities for incorporating what is sound in each of the other four models.[48] In 1987, however, he indicated a growing regard for the harmonizing capacities of the idea of the Church as "community of disciples."[49] Because of its attentiveness to both of these ideas, he admired the sentence skillfully crafted by the Extraordinary Synod of 1985: "The Church as communion is a sacrament for the salvation of the world."[50]

As mentioned earlier, Avery Dulles returned to the question of the purpose of the Church in his book *The Reshaping of Catholicism*, wanting on this, as on other issues, to draw afresh on the teaching of the Council. He turned specifically to *Gaudium et Spes*. There, the Council taught that Christ alone can solve the riddle of human existence, and said that, "in the light of Christ" it wanted to speak to all people and to "cooperate in finding a solution to the outstanding problems of our time" (GS 10). Despite that affirmation, Dulles notes that the Council was "surprisingly reserved" about its ability to give practical answers to those problems and stated that that was not directly its task. *Gaudium et Spes* 42 says that the "specific mission" (*missio propria*) given by Christ to the Church was not "in the political, economic or social order" but in the religious order. A footnote to GS 58 gives a pithy quotation from Pope Pius XI to make the point: "It is necessary never to lose sight of the fact that the objective of the Church is to evangelize, not to civilize. If it civilizes, it is by means of evangelization."[51]

Now, evangelization clearly concerns the outermost circle mentioned by Paul VI, namely, the secular realm. What about the two inner circles? There has often been debate as to whether evangelization is compatible with interreligious dialogue, and there would certainly be objections if ecumenical dialogue were simply classified as part of the Catholic Church's work of evangelization. There are extremely delicate issues here: What is the relationship between dialogue and evangelization? Are these not very different enterprises, both in fact and in principle? These issues, recently taken up by the Congregation for the Doctrine of the Faith,[52] have been pondered by Avery Dulles in the most recent phase of his writings.

THE RECENT PERIOD

The hallmark of this period is the idea of a "new evangelization," proclaimed by Pope John Paul II in his encyclical letter *Redemptoris Missio* (1990), and enthusiastically endorsed by Avery Dulles. Pope John Paul said, "I sense that the moment has come to commit all of the Church's energies to a new evangelization and to the mission *ad gentes*. No believer in Christ, no institution of the Church can avoid this supreme duty: to proclaim Christ to all peoples."[53] That is an all-encompassing commitment, and in 1992, Dulles gave a lengthy commentary on it:

> In my judgement, the evangelical vision of Popes Paul VI
> and John Paul II is one of the most surprising and impor-
> tant developments in the Catholic Church since Vatican II.
> This development…did not take place without a degree of

preparation in Vatican II and pre-conciliar kerygmatic theology. But Paul VI went beyond the council in identifying
evangelization with the total mission of the Church.[54] John
Paul II, with his unique familiarity with world Catholicism,
assigns the highest priority to evangelization in the mission
of the Church....All of this constitutes a remarkable shift in
the Catholic tradition. For centuries evangelization had
been a poor stepchild. Even when the term was used, evangelization was treated as a secondary matter, the special
vocation of a few priests and religious....Today we seem to
be witnessing the birth of a new Catholicism which, without loss of its institutional, sacramental and social dimensions, is authentically evangelical.[55]

In his encyclical, John Paul himself noted that many people think, since
Vatican II, that missionary work has been replaced by interreligious dialogue and is, therefore, now redundant.[56] He urged instead a perception
that "interreligious dialogue is a part of the Church's evangelizing mission."[57] Let us boldly ask, Might the same be true of *ecumenical* dialogue?
And if so, how?

The key to answering these questions lies in the fact that, as Dulles
notes in his 2003 address on "Ecumenism and Evangelization," John Paul
II, like Paul VI before him, actually had a very broad understanding of
evangelization.[58] Paul VI said, "The Church is an evangelizer, but she
begins by being evangelized herself,"[59] and John Paul said of every local
church that it is "both evangelized and evangelizing."[60] So evangelization
is for all, Catholics in the innermost circle included, and therefore *a for-
tiori*, we might say, it is for everyone in the three outer circles, including
our Christian brothers and sisters. The contact that we have with them,
and likewise that they have with us, is a means of *mutual evangelization*.

Dulles notes that John Paul identified "three situations" for evangelization, which merge into each other and are not "water-tight com-
partments": first, evangelization proper, where the gospel has never
been proclaimed; second, actual solid Christian communities exercis-
ing pastoral care for their members; and third, places where the faith
has grown cold and a reevangelization is needed.[61] As can be seen,

therefore, the "pastoral care" of active Christians falls within what Dulles calls the "comprehensive idea of evangelization" set forth by these recent popes,[62] and he himself attractively describes how ecumenical dialogue fits into the same picture. "The parties 'evangelize' one another," he says, "to the extent that they help one another to overcome their deficiencies and to accept authentic Christian elements that they had overlooked or neglected."[63] In other words, the "exchange of riches" of which he had spoken thirty years earlier[64] is a mutual evangelization.

There is, of course, another reason why any human contact should always, deep down, be a form of evangelization for a Christian, and that is because the life of God that is in us of its very nature goes out to others in love. There is in us a "divine compulsion"[65] to share what we have been given. We can do no other. "Woe to *me*," said Saint Paul to the Corinthians [note: not to *you*]: "Woe to me if I do not proclaim the gospel!" (1 Cor 9:16).[66]

> The church has become too introverted. If Catholics today are sometimes weak in their faith, this is partly because of their reluctance to share it. Unless the Gospel message were a truth to be communicated to others, it would not be of great value for believers themselves. Once we grasp the universal validity of the message and its significance for the whole of human life, we gain anew appreciation of the privilege of being its bearers and a new eagerness to share it. As John Paul II asserts: "Faith is strengthened when it is given to others."[67]

In 2007, in a vivid address describing six "Models of Evangelization," with many colorful examples, Dulles ended with that same quotation from John Paul II and with its converse: "faith," he said, "is weakened when we hoard it to ourselves."[68]

He himself certainly did not do that, and those whom he admired, in recent times perhaps especially Pope John Paul II,[69] have not either. Dulles's magisterial *History of Apologetics*, dating from 1971 and recently republished, tells the story, as he says, of so many "thoughtful Christians," who, "in different ages and cultures, have striven to 'give a reason for the hope that was in them' (cf. 1 Pet 3:15)."[70] All of them are *models of evangelization*, as of course is he. We are reminded of a line from Henri de Lubac, who is given several honorable mentions in the *History*: "If I no longer feel the need to communicate the flame, it is because it no longer burns in me....To give is to participate in the divine Life which is Gift."[71] It is a privilege to honor the flame that has burned—and burns still—in Avery Cardinal Dulles.

3

A TALE OF
TWO CARDINALS

Robert Barron

E ven the most cursory glance at the work of Avery Cardinal Dulles
reveals the influence of John Henry Newman. So many of
Newman's major themes—faith and reason, theological method, religious epistemology, apologetics, ecumenism—are Dulles's principal
preoccupations. Newman is one of the most cited authorities in the
writings of Dulles, but what is perhaps most remarkable is how
Newman's thought, even when not explicitly averred to, functions so
consistently as a structuring element in Dulles's speculations. Moreover,
as many have pointed out, there is a fascinating analogy between the
lives and careers of these two princes of the Church. Both were con-
verts from Protestantism—Newman from High Anglicanism and
Dulles from Presbyterianism—both pursued careers as distinguished
university scholars, both were public intellectuals and controversialists,
both curiously transcended the customary categories of left and right,
and both became cardinals in their later years. In this chapter, we will
explore just two major areas in which Avery Dulles incorporated and
developed the thought of John Henry Newman: the nature of religious
epistemology, and the tensive play between ecclesiastical authority and
theology. Hopefully, this proves more than simply an academic exercise, for I am convinced that the way that Cardinal Dulles used Cardinal
Newman is especially clarifying regarding some of the ecclesial and
intellectual problems that bedevil us today.

RELIGIOUS EPISTEMOLOGY

Throughout his career, John Henry Newman opposed the frontal assaults of the avatars of Enlightenment reason against the bulwark of classical Christianity, but it is fascinating to observe that he did not do so through an intellectual retrenchment, a retreat into premodern styles of argument. Rather, in a manner remarkably anticipatory of the postmodernists of the twentieth century, he demonstrated the limitations, blind spots, and aporias of Enlightenment reason itself. This Newman-style engagement of the modern critics of Christianity is on full display in Cardinal Dulles's meditations on postcritical theology in his 1992 text *The Craft of Theology*.

On Dulles's reading, the properly critical period commenced with the overthrowing of the authority of Aristotle in the realm of science, effected by Bacon, Galileo, and others. It was then given philosophical form and specificity through the work of Descartes and Spinoza.[1] Descartes's strategy in the *Discourse on Method*—the bracketing of all received moral and intellectual traditions in the interest of finding an indubitable foundation for knowledge—became paradigmatic for practically all modern philosophy. If Descartes's and Spinoza's form of epistemological foundationalism was intuitional and rational, that of John Locke and David Hume could be characterized as empirical. Those influential British philosophers engaged in a similar skeptical bracketing of traditional claims to certitude but averred that all legitimate knowledge was based, not so much in Cartesian intuitions, but in direct perception, or the memory of direct perception.

Now philosophers from both camps articulated a form of rational religion justifiable precisely on these foundationalist grounds. (The explicit atheism of Feuerbach, Nietzsche, Marx, and Freud would develop later.) Malebranche, Spinoza, Kant, and Descartes all presented versions of religion rooted in self-evident first principles; Locke offered an empirically verifiable religion in his *Reasonableness of Christianity*, and many Deists followed his lead.

Many intelligent Christians of the eighteenth and nineteenth centuries perceived, of course, that these new rationalist construals of biblical religion undermined the dogmatic structure of a properly revealed faith, and they reacted accordingly. One has only to consult the condemnations of rationalism in both the *Syllabus of Errors* and the official documents of Vatican I to see a Catholic version of this resistance. However, Cardinal Dulles points out that the scholasticism of this period, though used ostensibly to counteract the foundationalist rationalism of the Enlightenment, mimicked and mirrored that very form of thought. In a manner quite alien to Aquinas, the scholastics of the time searched for indubitable rational grounds for belief, clinching arguments upon which the claims of faith could be based: "The neo-scholastic theology of the nineteenth and early twentieth centuries...was heavily infected by Cartesian rationalism and mathematicism."[2]

Of course, a second path lay open to thoughtful Christians as they contemplated the critiques of the moderns, and this was to adopt the modern method explicitly and to ground the claims of Christianity in something like self-evident intuitions. The most influential and important practitioner of this approach was Friedrich Schleiermacher, who met the cultured despisers of religion with the mollifying observation that the dogmas and doctrines of classical Christianity were but symbolic manifestations of the underlying and universally held feeling of absolute dependency. In this, he proposed a religious version of the Cartesian *cogito*. The Schleiermacherian style proved very popular among academic theologians in the nineteenth and early twentieth centuries, inspiring the projects of, among many others, Ritschl, Otto, Tillich, and Rahner.

Over the past two hundred years, critics have consistently argued that very few of the cultured despisers of Christianity have, in fact, been persuaded by Schleiermacher and his disciples, and, more importantly, that his subjectivist epistemology has resulted in a fatal positioning of revelation by neutral psychological experience. The theological projects of Karl Barth and Hans Urs von Balthasar, for instance, center around a critique of Schleiermacher's method. It appeared, therefore, that the engagement with modernity on the part of Christians—either to blame it or to praise it—resulted in a problematic compromise with it.

But Avery Dulles points out that, in the middle of the twentieth century, a new approach began to emerge, one that might be characterized as postmodern or postcritical. In a philosophical context, Ludwig Wittgenstein, Paul-Michel Foucault, Hans-Georg Gadamer, and Michael

Polanyi were the key players, and among the theologians, Hans Urs von Balthasar and George Lindbeck led the way.[3] Over and against the rationalism and subjectivism of the Cartesian school, these thinkers emphasized the importance of the nonrational and the prerational in every concrete act of knowing. For example, Gadamer argued that prejudice necessarily played a constructive role in the commencement of any conversation or the interpretation of any text. What the Cartesians tried desperately to eliminate—unexamined tradition, prerational conviction, preconception—Gadamer blithely reinstated.[4] In fact, he argued that the *cogito* itself would be impossible without a complete set of assumptions and linguistic conventions accepted, perforce, without definitive proof.

For his part, Foucault delighted in demonstrating the often brutal and irrational motivations that animated the purportedly enlightened social practices of early and late modernity. Following Wittgenstein here, Lindbeck insisted that certain communal practices and a definite form of life inevitably shaped the consciousness of even the most isolated and skeptical Cartesian knower.[5] In all these ways, the postmodernists questioned the pretentions of modern reason to be critical, neutral, untainted by ungrounded convictions.

Cardinal Dulles associated himself with this postcritical style and urged that it be used in the formulation of a proper theological method. In a sense, the adoption of this new approach would allow the Christian theologian to cut the Gordian knot of the modern problem and to articulate the faith without being positioned by liberal assumptions. With the help of Polyani, Dulles lays out several basic aspects of this approach. First, whereas the critical or modern method was "animated by a bias toward doubt...with the implied assumption that the royal road to truth consists in uprooting all voluntary commitments," the postcritical program commences with a kind of prejudice in favor of faith and the adoption of a hermeneutic of trust rather than suspicion.[6] If the Cartesian attitude was understandable in the period following the wars of religion, it is, Dulles argues, a distinct liability now "when moral and religious convictions have been thoroughly eroded by skepticism."

Second, Dulles comments, in a Gadamerian vein, that the critical program, formed by modern skepticism, itself rested on a fiduciary basis—a whole network of assumptions and convictions such as "the postulates of Euclidean geometry and the testimony of the senses." Here, one thinks of the standard postmodern observation that every act of sensible perception is theory laden rather than neutral.

Third, Dulles holds that "it is impossible to apply the critical program consistently," precisely because systematic doubt is "repugnant to human nature."[7] Since we do not have anything approaching apodictic proof for even the most ordinary facts of experience—the existence of an external world, the "reliability of physical and behavioral laws," the forward progress of time—we cannot possibly endure over the long haul the epistemic asceticism that Descartes requires. One thinks here of Jacques Maritain's famous critique of the implicit "angelism" in much of modern epistemology and anthropology.

Fourth, Cardinal Dulles observes that the strict critical program overlooks the necessarily social dimension of even the simplest act of knowing.[8] Upon reading Descartes, Spinoza, or Kant, one has the impression that authentic knowledge can be achieved by the individual in isolation from his community and from his tradition. However, those paradigmatically modern thinkers themselves were, in fact, massively shaped by the conversations they had with both the living and the dead, the *cogito* necessarily giving way to the *cogitamus*.

Fifth, and most fundamentally, Dulles maintains that "the critical program overlooked the tacit dimension of knowledge," giving no "cognitive value to what Pascal meant by 'the reasons of the heart.'" Does one know best in a detached, objective, basically disinterested manner; or does one know most effectively through a subtly interlocked weave of analysis, instinct, feel, and passion? To opt for the latter position is to be postcritical. In her *Upheavals of Thought*, Martha Nussbaum convincingly showed how her fiercely emotional reaction to the news of her mother's death carried an epistemic valence, telling her truths about her mother and their relationship that objectively analytical reason never could.[9] To construe emotion as merely expressive or to consign it to the level of the irrational is, for the postcritical Nussbaum, fatally to overlook the role that it plays in coming to know the truth of things.

In making these claims, Dulles shows himself a disciple, not only of Michael Polanyi, but very much of John Henry Newman. As suggested previously, Newman was, if we may put it this way, proto-postmodern or proto-postcritical in his approach, and, regarding the program just out-lined, a significant forerunner. In his masterpiece of his late career, *The Grammar of Assent*, Newman explicitly took on the empirical founda-tionalism of John Locke. In his epistemological writings, Locke had argued that, were philosophy and science to remain responsible and not bogged down by obscurantism and superstition, assent and inference ought to be tightly correlated. This means that the act of accepting a proposition as true ought to have a valence coordinated with the quality of argument used to justify it, so that if the evidence for a given propo-sition is clinching, the assent to it ought to be absolute, and if the evi-dence is less persuasive, the assent should be mitigated, and so on. To do otherwise, Locke insisted, was to be, not only intellectually suspect, but morally blameworthy as well.[10]

Newman, who deeply admired Locke, admitted that syllogistic or strictly demonstrative ratiocination plays an essential role in bringing the mind to assent, but he insisted, over and against Locke, that the act of assenting ought never to be coordinated reductively to the quality of inferential support. While syllogisms often point correctly in the direc-tion of truth, they are in themselves typically inconclusive, since they commence with generalizations that cannot reach to particular cases. "All men have a price; Fabricius is a man; therefore, Fabricius has a price," is valid reasoning precisely in the measure that the peculiarities of Fabricius are subsumed under the umbrella term *man*, but Fabricius just might be that one peculiar man who does not have a price. The upshot of this is that assent is often, even typically, given independently of strict inference. Sometimes, Newman said, "men are loud in their admiration of truths which they never profess;" or to turn it around, some people will assent enthusiastically to propositions for which there are, at best, very bad arguments.[11]

In regard to the way that human beings actually come to assent, formal inference—what Locke insisted upon—is supplemented by what Newman called informal inference, that is, the whole range of hunches, intuitions, experiences, suppositions "too fine to avail separately, too sub-tle and circuitous to be convertible into syllogisms."[12] In Newman's famous example, one comes to assent unhesitatingly to the proposition that Great Britain is an island through certain kinds of formal inference complemented by a number of prerational or nonrational hints: every map of Europe represents Great Britain as an island; the entire written history of the country assumes this insularity; every reasonable person that one converses with takes it for granted; one's own explorations confirm it, and so on. For the instinct of the mind that governs the process of informal inference, Newman coined the term "illative sense," from the Latin *ferre, latus*, "to carry." The illative sense is the epistemic counterpart to *phronesis* in the moral life, for both constitute a feel for the particular, for this pointed judgment of truth in the one case, and for moral rectitude in the other. It is an intuition for the trajectory of converging probable arguments.

Considering these insights from *The Grammar of Assent*, let's now return to the five qualities of a postcritical method and note their resonance with Newman's theory. Dulles's postcritical approach, as we saw, favors faith and rests upon a hermeneutic of trust rather than one of suspicion. Newman takes for granted that, due to the illative sense, the clear majority of people are untroubled in the assents that they make to myriad propositions for which there is no clinching inferential support, and he assumes that few of them could even begin to articulate with rational clarity precisely why it is that they make such confident intellectual moves. He cites with approval the adage that a good judge should hand down his decisions firmly and confidently, but that he should resist the temptation to give the reasons for those decisions, for his judgments are undoubtedly correct, though the justifications are largely unknown, even to him. What does this represent but a hermeneutic of trust regarding ordinary (and not so ordinary) moves of the mind?

Next, Dulles's postcritical epistemology assumes that a "fiduciary" basis remains in place even for the most disinterested, neutral, and "objective" intellectual projects. Newman argues in the *Grammar of Assent* that we regularly assent to the "furniture of the mind," that full range of basic assumptions concerning experience, the laws of nature, the syntax of language, and so on, though, once again, we can summon nothing like apodictic arguments on their behalf. When Descartes, in that heated room in Ulm, formulated and executed his program of systematic doubt, he could not, even in principle, seriously doubt the furniture of his mind, especially language itself, which made the doubting possible.[13] In his study of Newman, Dulles reminds us that "in his own day, Newman felt called upon to combat the myth of an autonomous realm in which reason, operating without presumptions, would deliver uncontestable conclusions. He showed that, in concrete matters, reason always depends upon presumptions, and that these presumptions are by no means self-evident."[14]

Third, we saw that Dulles's postcritical method resists the angelism that suggests that radical doubt can be seriously sustained. In the *Grammar of Assent*, Newman explicitly scores Locke for just this sort of angelism, when he argues that perhaps in a higher world inference and assent are as tightly correlated, as Locke says they should be, but that here below, real human beings do not countenance so rigorous a correspondence. Indeed, one could argue easily enough that were the Lockean recommendation followed faithfully, we would give confident assent to practically nothing at all. Newman counters Locke, not deductively and abstractly, or even on "moral" grounds, but pragmatically, insisting that real, embodied people just do not think this way.

We recall that the fifth and final feature of Dulles's postcritical method was an insistence on the tacit dimension of knowing, all the ways that the reasons of the heart involve themselves in the process of coming to assent. The illative sense is nothing but the faculty for sorting through and assessing precisely these nonrational intuitions and perceptions. In this regard, Pascal's *raisons du coeur* meet Newman's *cor ad cor loquitur*, and both clearly inform Avery Dulles's postcritical epistemology.[15]

To explore Newman's influence on the fourth of Dulles's principles, we must leave the confines of the *Grammar of Assent* and consult Newman's mid-career work, *An Essay on the Development of Christian Doctrine*. It is in the context of this treatment of the living quality of ideas that the *cogitamus* dimension of knowing comes most clearly to the fore. In line with the *Lebensphilosophie* of the period, Newman insisted that a real idea is never a static given, a fixed Platonic form. Rather, he argued, ideas exist neither in a transcendent realm nor on the printed page but in "the play of lively minds."[16] Whereas Hume held that the mind is a kind of empty theatre in which impressions and sense data appear for neutral viewing, Newman opined that human intelligence is a lively, active, inquisitive power, constantly sifting and weighing evidence, making judgments, asking and answering questions. It should come as no surprise that Lonergan's analysis of the highly energized agent intellect in *Insight* should have come after multiple readings of Newman's epistemology.

This restive intellectual process obtains not simply within the individual mind but also intersubjectively in the play of conversation and debate. One thinker tosses an idea, already refined and analyzed, to an interlocutor, who turns it, wonders at it, further refines it, and then passes it to another thinker who does the same. Newman compares this conversational development of the idea to the unfolding and deepening of a river over time.[17] Remarkably anticipating Husserlian phenomenology, Newman comments that a real idea is equivalent to the sum total of its possible aspects.[18] Just as an adequate representation of a physical object, say the Sears Tower, would have to include a range of profiles, perspectives, and aspects, so even a relatively adequate understanding of an idea would have to include a startling number of that notion's dimensions. Therefore, real understanding rarely takes place in a flash of intuition but rather gradually, in the play of analysis and conversation, stretching across both space and time. But this means that the individual thinker, isolated in the confines of his subjectivity—in a word, the ideal Cartesian philosopher—is by no means the optimal knower. Rather, it is the one who situates himself within the context of a lively conversational community who will know best.

As noted, Newman is implicitly critical here of Descartes and his disciples, but he is critical as well of Luther and his followers, those who would maintain that the individual, in isolation from the believing community across the ages, can come to a sure grasp of the complex ideas that make up the Christian creed. In a word, Protestant "private judgment" strikes Newman as epistemologically counterindicated. We recall that the fourth of Dulles's postcritical principles was precisely a prejudice in favor of the social dimension of every act of knowing. Hopefully, it is clear that this prejudice could not be more Newmanesque.

PLAY BETWEEN MAGISTERIUM AND THEOLOGY

A theme that both John Henry Newman and Avery Dulles touched upon frequently in their writings was that of the tensive play between ecclesial authority and theological freedom. Both wrote during roiled times, when authority, both secular and sacred, was being questioned vigorously and when the claims of intellectual freedom were being pressed with vehemence. Avery Dulles did some of his most seminal and influential work during the 1960s and 1970s, precisely when the tension between ecclesiastical authority and academic liberty came to a head over issues of sexual morality. One has only to think of the two waves of the Charles Curran dispute, the first of which took place just after the publication of *Humanae Vitae*, and the second of which unfolded during Cardinal Dulles's years as Curran's professorial colleague at the Catholic University of America. Dulles's analysis of this thorny problem bears everywhere the mark of John Henry Newman's influence, especially in its balance and its keen sense of history.

Newman argued, throughout his career, that precisely because Christian ideas exist in the intersubjective play of lively minds, doctrine naturally develops, implicit dimensions of key notions becoming explicit only gradually. Cardinal Dulles shares this same perspective: "The message of Christ has to be proclaimed in new situations and interpreted for new audiences who have their own perspectives and their own questions."[19] Just as the oak tree is implicit in, but by no means reducible to, the acorn, so, for example, the fully unfolded idea of the incarnation is grounded in but not simply identical to the biblical stories and reflections concerning Jesus's identity. Therefore, the Protestant principle of *sola scriptura* struck Newman as deeply inadequate. Though the notion of doctrinal development strikes the contemporary reader as relatively liberal, for Newman it was in service of a defense of Catholic doctrines and practices that seemed, to many of his own contemporaries, aberrational. Thus, Newman managed successfully to hold off both a doctrinaire conservatism that would imagine Christian ideas as simply a deposit handed on unchanged from generation to generation and an undisciplined liberalism that would construe doctrine in a purely relativistic manner.

However, Newman perceived something else in this context, and it constitutes one of the greatest strokes of genius in his work. He noticed that ecclesiastical authority is a concomitant and not an opponent of doctrinal development, that the two ideas, so often seen as mutually exclusive are, in fact, mutually implicative. As in nature, so in the intellectual order, development can be either positive or negative. A body can unfold in such a way that its essential integrity and orderly functioning are compromised, and an idea can develop in a manner incongruent with its proper nature. In the first case, a physician capable of diagnosing the problem and dealing with it effectively is required for the health of the body; and in the second case, an authority capable of discerning ideational corruption and of dealing decisively with it is requisite for the healthy development of a doctrine.

From his youth, Newman knew that the Bible, open to such a wide variety of interpretations, could not be this authority. Dulles emphatically agrees with this: "Scripture alone, however, was never intended to be, and has not proved to be, a self-sufficient rule of faith."[20] When he was an Anglican, Newman held that antiquity (roughly the consensus of the greatest fathers) could serve this evaluating function, but as he was making the turn to Catholicism, he realized that the words of the fathers, however moving and truthful they were, could never function as a living voice, and hence could not definitively adjudicate disputes regarding development and corruption.

At the close of the *Apologia pro vita sua*, in his general answer to Mr. Kingsley, Newman maintains that the presence of an infallible ecclesiastical authority follows logically from the very idea of revelation.[21] If God revealed certain truths necessary for salvation, and if doctrine unfolds somewhat unpredictably and precariously over time, then it follows that God must provide for an authority sufficiently strong and clear to guarantee the integrity of those truths. Furthermore, this authority must be active, infallible, and personal if it is to have the required effect.

If I may shift the metaphor from the organic to the sociological, doctrinal development is like a game, and ecclesial authority like a referee. No basketball team has ever brought the ball up the court in precisely the same way, and each individual game unfolds in a distinctive manner, but integral play is presided over by a judge, whose purpose is the enforcement of the rules and the maintenance of the game's essential form. Precisely because the play flows, the authority of the referee is required, and precisely because the game is current and lively, the referee must have a voice and it must be definitive in its pronouncements.

In *The Craft of Theology*, Dulles articulates the role of the magisterium in a distinctly Newmanesque way: "The Church, as the bearer and interpreter of revelation, has the capacity to approve what is consonant with, or reject what is dissonant with, the word entrusted to it. The organ that authoritatively expresses the mind of the Church is known as the ecclesiastical magisterium."[22] Again, this role is required, not to keep doctrine from developing, but to monitor and encourage healthy development.

Newman was obliged to engage the objections of his skeptical contemporaries who worried that the acceptance of an infallible ecclesiastical authority would imply the intellectual subservience of humanity, a retreat into premodern obscurantism. He responded, in the *Apologia*, with this remarkable statement:"The energy of the human intellect does from opposition grow; it thrives and is joyous with a tough elastic strength under the terrible blows of the divinely-fashioned weapon and is never so much itself as when it has lately been overthrown."[23] Just as the energy and verve of a river come from its firm banks and just as the excitement of an athletic competition is made possible by the unbending quality of the game's rules and obstacles, so the effervescence and creativity of the intellect are grounded in the very limits set to it. Without defined banks, the swift-flowing river would devolve into a lazy lake; without borders infallibly defined, the theological mind, Newman holds, would devolve into idle speculation and relativism.

David Tracy has argued that the theological community can, through critique, peer review, book reviews, and so on, effectively police itself, free from the interference of ecclesial authority, which is seen today, at least in the West, as arbitrary and invasive. Newman would have little patience with that position. Asking theologians to monitor their own discussions would be akin to asking baseball players to umpire their own game. Paul commented that his apostolic authority was given to him "to edification and not to destruction," and in this Newman finds the perfect characterization of ecclesial authority's role vis-à-vis theological investigation: "Its object is not to enfeeble freedom or vigor of human thought in religious speculation, but to resist and control its extravagance."[24]

Once again, Cardinal Dulles concurs with this basic line of thought. Commenting on the regnant perception of the rapport between magisterium and theology, Dulles says, "Tensions can arise between the hierarchical authorities and theologians. From some literature, one gets the impression that the two groups are engaged in a perpetual contest, and that every advance of one group is achieved at the expense of the other. The magisterium, according to this scenario, would be asking theologians to 'knuckle under' to abandon their own judgment and sacrifice the integrity of their own discipline....This journalistic portrayal of the relationship is a caricature."[25] For both Dulles and Newman, the play of magisterium and theology is not a zero-sum game, but rather a tensely harmonic relationship.

What, for Newman, are the limits to ecclesiastical authority? What prevents it from morphing into authoritarianism? A first restriction is that the Church's infallibility ought not to extend beyond the definite circle formed by the moral law, the principles of natural religion, and the apostolic faith.[26] If it tries to assert itself outside this relatively narrow range, or if it seeks too precisely to determine the concrete implications of these foundations, it oversteps. Furthermore, the official teaching authority of the Church—the pope in union with an ecumenical council—has existed only a relatively few times in the long history of the Church. And the extraordinary magisterium involving a papal statement *ex cathedra* had, in Newman's time, been invoked precisely once, in the declaration of Mary's immaculate conception.

The point, here, is that the awful power of infallible definition is employed only carefully and rarely, lest it interrupt unnecessarily the healthy flow of the theological conversation. Just as a bad referee can intervene too frequently in the game and hence compromise its natural rhythm, so the ecclesial authority can hover too fussily over the give and take, the experimentation and speculation, involved in doctrinal development. In the *Apologia*, Newman avers that a theologian or apologist, wishing to forward a new idea that he considers helpful for his day, welcomes the opportunity to write, to think, to debate, and to launch his views into the public forum. He would be cowed into inaction were he to feel that "an authority, which was supreme and final, was watching every word he said and making signs of assent or dissent to each sentence as he uttered it."[27]

In his meditations on the prudential norms that ought to govern the utterances of the magisterium, Avery Dulles observes that "until the twentieth century, ecumenical councils and dogmatic decrees were rare. Popes issued relatively few doctrinal decisions and then only at the end of a long process of theological discussion."[28] He continues, very much in the spirit of John Henry Newman: "Unless the authorities exercise great restraint, Catholics can easily feel overwhelmed by the multitude of views they are expected to profess....Wherever diversity seems to be tolerable, theologians and others should be given freedom to use their own good judgment."[29] Finally, he invokes Newman directly: "Newman and, later, Pope John XXIII were fond of the ancient dictum: *In necessariis unitas, in dubiis libertas, in omnibus caritas.*"[30]

Stressing the importance of a lengthy process of intellectual sifting, largely uninterrupted by interventions of ecclesial authority, Dulles shows himself, again, a disciple of Newman. In the *Apologia,* the nineteenth-century cardinal gives a rich description of the gradual steps by which a controverted theological question comes, at long last, to be adjudicated by the highest ecclesiastical court. He observes that a controversial position might be defended by a local preacher or professor, and the question allowed to smolder and burn, while Rome takes no action. Eventually, the issue might be taken up by a professor at another seat of learning, where it is mulled over while Rome takes no action. Next, it may be formally condemned by a theological faculty of a major university, and still Rome remains silent. If the question continues to be divisive, the local ordinary might attempt to resolve it, while Rome does nothing. Finally, only if he is unsuccessful, might the bishop present the matter to the Roman doctrinal authorities for their judgment.[31] The very salutary thing that has happened in this long and slow process is that the issue has been so weighed, considered, turned over, and seen from multiple perspectives that, when Rome makes its decision, it is usually but a ratification of the truth that has already emerged. Dulles's conclusion is very close in spirit to that of Newman: "The magisterium can avoid issuing too many statements, especially statements that appear to carry with them an obligation to assent."[32]

John Henry Newman articulates a final restriction on the potentially tyrannical exercise of ecclesiastical authority, namely, the inescapable dependence of that authority on the work and expertise of the theological community. Newman makes the keen historical observation that the great formulators of doctrine have not, for the most part, been popes, bishops, and magisterial officials. "Authority in its most imposing exhibition, grave bishops laden with the traditions and rivalries of particular nations or places, have been guided in their decisions by the commanding genius of individuals, sometimes young and of inferior rank."[33] Thus, Origen, Irenaeus, Tertullian, and Augustine formed the mind of the ancient Church more than any pope, and their teachings grounded the decisions of the great early councils. Thomas Aquinas, a humble Dominican friar, had the profoundest impact on the shaping of the medieval Church, and his formulations significantly shaped the statements of the Council of Trent on original sin, justification, and the sacraments. One of Newman's heroes, the young deacon Athanasius, gave form to the Church's eventual magisterial determinations against Arianism. Newman's overall point is that the infallible teaching office of the Church, far from putting theological creativity to bed, positively calls it forth and relies upon it.

Once more, Avery Dulles could not be in more enthusiastic agreement with his cardinalatial predecessor. In *The Craft of Theology*, he shows this dependence of authority upon theology in even greater historical detail than Newman. "What would the documents of Trent look like had it not been for the work of papal theologians such as Lainez and Salmeron? What would Vatican I have been able to say without the preparatory texts supplied by Franzelin, Kleutgen, and others? How would Vatican II have been able to accomplish its task in the absence of Congar, Phillips, Rahner, Murray, and their colleagues?"[34] He goes on to comment that nearly every papal encyclical was made possible through the efforts of theologians who prepared drafts and responded to questions and that no Roman congregation or episcopal doctrinal commission could do its work without the contribution of numerous theological researchers. Moreover, Dulles insists that theologians are indispensable to the proper interpretation and reception of dogmatic statements uttered by the magisterium. Dulles thereby makes his own Rahner's observation that every doctrinal statement of the Church is, in one sense, an end to discussion, but, in another sense, very much a beginning of further conversation, clarification, and interpretation.

CONCLUSION

In his intellectual autobiography, *A Testimonial to Grace*, Cardinal Dulles gives us a gripping account of his journey from a somewhat world-weary materialism to a vibrantly imagined Catholic faith. To be sure, there was a powerfully academic dimension to this itinerary. To give just one example, Dulles's reading of Plato and Aristotle when he was still a collegian played a decisive role in moving him to accept the ideas of order in nature, final causality, and objective morality, all of which would prove decisive in his eventual conversion to the faith. However, in one of the most lyrical passages in the book, Cardinal Dulles describes how he first came to give what Newman would have called "real assent" to the idea of God, and this involved much more than mere reason. He speaks of a walk that he took one gray February afternoon when he was an undergraduate at Harvard:

> As I wandered aimlessly, something impelled me to look contemplatively at a young tree. On its frail, supple branches were young buds attending eagerly the spring which was at hand. While my eye rested upon them the thought came to me suddenly...that these little buds in their innocence and meekness followed a rule, a law of which I as yet knew nothing. How could it be, I asked, that this delicate tree sprang up and developed and that all the enormous complexity of its cellular operations combined to make it grow erectly and bring forth leaves and blossoms? The answer was new to me: that its actions were ordered to an end by the

only power capable of adapting means to ends…a Person of whom I had no previous intuition.[35]

This lengthy quotation discloses so beautifully a Newmanesque account of assent. There was undoubtedly an intellectual aspect to this coming to see (inferential reason was clearly operative), but there was something else as well. There was beauty, the quality of the day and time, the pensive mood in which the young searcher found himself, that specific tree with its early spring buds—and all these elements and many others came together, along with formal ratiocination to produce the moment of breakthrough and vision that Cardinal Dulles describes. What guided this rational and other than rational process was none other than Newman's illative sense. It is my conviction that an apologetics for a postcritical age will involve just this sort of confident use of both the rational and the affective, both the discursive and the intuitive, both the theological and the artistic in the process of bringing people to faith. Both John Henry Newman and Avery Dulles witnessed to this truth.

In the 1966 edition of *A Testimonial to Grace*, Cardinal Dulles adds a chapter on the present situation in the Church. He acknowledges that the intellectual acumen of the theological community, in seminaries, universities, and other institutions of higher learning has, perhaps, never been greater. Theology in one sense is vital and creative. However, he observes as well that the relationship between theology and the magisterium has become strained and tendentious. He says that central teachings of Vatican II on the role of the pope and bishops, the divine constitution of the Church, the necessity of the sacraments, and so on, are "widely contested or ignored" in the theological community.[36] Furthermore, many in the West consider the Church a purely human society, capable of changing its structure and teaching at the whim of the faithful, much as a modern political state can change its leaders and constitution through majority vote. This falling apart of creative theology and authoritative magisterium has led to a polarization and politicization of the life of the Church, giving rise to the battles between liberal and conservative Catholics. Cardinal Dulles sees this split as one of the bitterest fruits of the postconciliar period and insists that only when it is healed will the Church regain the confidence and balance necessary for effective evangelization. No theologian would be more helpful in this regard than John Henry Newman.

The new evangelization will depend greatly upon the right understanding of both religious epistemology and the rapport between theology and authority. I hope that this tale of two cardinals has contributed, however modestly, to that understanding.

4

VATICAN II AND UNDERSTANDING REVELATION[1]

Emery de Gaál

It was an altogether improbable turn of events: the Presbyterian son of a future U.S. secretary of state, the grandson and great-grandnephew of former U.S. secretaries of state, the nephew of a CIA director, and the grandson of a liberal Presbyterian theologian converted on November 26, 1940, to Catholicism.[2] How could a scion of a patrician family, trained in one of the best nonsectarian boarding schools of New England,[3] acquainted with the cosmopolitan ambience of a Swiss secondary education, having imbibed the positivism of Auguste Comte[4] and exposed to the prevailing currents of skepticism, materialism, liberalism, and even outright atheism,[5] find in Catholicism the fulfillment of all his ideals and hopes, the most profound and truest response to all the investigations of the human intellect into the origin and purpose of human existence?

At the beginning of modern theology stands a towering figure, seemingly denying apodictically the future of any kind of theology: Immanuel Kant. He maintained that nothing speculative can be stated of God or any other nonmaterial reality. The range of the human mind is limited to sense experience alone. Ever since, modern epistemology subverts the critical distinction between revealed and acquired knowledge.[6] Thus the Christian notion of revelation seems to have been dealt a death knell. To this, "the church father of modern theology," Friedrich Schleiermacher, obliged famously by arguing that if positive revelation does not stand a chance in the court of reason, then religion is but feeling and taste for the infinite. Thus, to him "dogmatic theology is the science which systematizes the doctrine *prevalent* in a Christian Church *at a given time*."[7] Ergo, significant representatives of modernity reject any Thomistic notion of the *analogia entis*, analogy of being, and are beholden to enlightened agnosticism.

Can Catholic theology overcome this *garstigen Graben*, this "nasty ditch" between the phenomenal and noumenal realms—to use a phrase Kant's contemporaries coined? Along the lines provided by the Second Vatican Council's Dogmatic Constitution on Divine Revelation, *Dei Verbum*, and going well beyond these, the priest and theologian Avery Dulles achieved this feat.

A good and credible—and therefore over the ages enduring—theology is always biographical and classical. This means it must be based on a personal faith experience placed at the disposition of the Church so that it might edify the people of God. Avery Cardinal Dulles was granted such a foundational experience of faith at the beginning of his adult life that would find subsequently theoretical adumbration and consecution most prominently in his reflections on the nature of revelation. Indeed, there is no gainsaying, as Dermot Lane observes: Dulles's achievements in the area of revelation are "the most comprehensive treatment on revelation in the English-speaking world."[8] The personal experience of revelation and his remarkable contributions to theology find their common underlying, forward impelling motif in the motto he chose upon being created cardinal by John Paul II of blessed memory in the year 2001: *Scio cui credidi*—"I know the one in whom I have put my trust" (2 Tim 1:12).[9]

PROLEGOMENA

Writing in early fall of 1944, soon after his entry into the Catholic Church, as a navy lieutenant on board the cruiser *U.S.S. Philadelphia*, his first religious book, *A Testimonial to Grace*, which he considered foundational for his later theological endeavors,[10] and with memories of his conversion still vivid, he states,

My philosophy failed me because it was not big enough to contain the human, let alone the heroic. By an odd paradox, I noted, man could find no joy unless he sought it not, unless he lived by love, which 'seeketh not her own.' Was there, I asked, some other good, above and apart from the human enjoyment, capable of eliciting the boundless resources of devotion, loyalty and fortitude which lay dormant in the soul? Was there some end sufficiently exalted to justify great undertakings and to deploy in all their splendor the faculties of mind and character with which man is endowed?....The barren desolation of my materialist philosophy, its utter falseness and my humiliation at discovering it so, gave God His chance.[11]

In Harvard's Widener Library, he had been pouring over a chapter of Augustine's *De Civitate Dei*, which had been assigned as a reading in one of his courses in medieval history. He writes,

On an impulse I closed the book; I was irresistibly prompted to go out into the open air. It was a bleak, rainy day, rather warm for the time of year. The slush of melting snow formed a deep mud along the banks of the River Charles, which I followed down towards Boston. I enjoyed the cool rain in my face and the melancholy of the scene. As I wandered aimlessly, something impelled me to look contemplatively at a young tree....[when] the thought came to me suddenly, with all the strength and novelty of a revelation, that these little buds in their innocence and meekness followed a rule, a law of which I as yet knew nothing....[their] actions were ordered to an end by the only power capable of adapting means to ends—intelligence—and that the very fact that this intelligence worked toward an end implied purposiveness—in other words, a will....As I turned home that evening, the darkness closing around, I was conscious that I had discovered something which would introduce me to a new life, set off by a sharp hiatus from the past.

That night, for the first time in years, I prayed. I knelt down in the chill blankness...and attempted to raise my heart and mind toward Him of Whose presence and power I had become so unexpectedly aware. I recited the Our Father....

Never, since the eventful day which I have described, have I doubted the existence of an all-good and omnipotent God. Now all the proofs of God's existence carried no weight for Dulles. His acceptance of God's existence "rested on something like an intuition...and as such I find it partly incommunicable."[12]

Well before writing his book on revelation, he writes as a nontheologian on this germane topic, while balancing a typewriter on the choppy waters during the Battle of the Atlantic. Concerning the parables of Our Lord, "they were so rich in doctrine and symbolism that the most learned could not exhaust their subtle moral implications, their wealth of dogma and their deep prophetic meaning."[13] As divine incarnation, the life of Jesus is the self-expression of the Eternal in time.

Astonishingly, by choosing the words *doctrine* and *symbolism* with yet no theological training but anticipating *Dei Verbum* by twenty years and almost forty years before composing his magisterial book *Models of Revelation*, Dulles was already mindful of a critical balance between propositional truth and the symbolic nature of revelation.[14]

LAYING THE INTELLECTUAL FOUNDATIONS

What were the factors that led to this amazing discovery? First and foremost, these are existential veracity and—as he admits—"intellectual honesty" but, above all—as he phrases it—"solely...the grace of God."[15] The eclectic potpourri of his ancestral Presbyterian Church and the other Protestant denominations' failure to insist on the inerrancy of doctrine as inherited from Jesus Christ certainly contributed. As a result, reciting the Apostles' Creed in Protestant congregations had become hollow and the sermons delivered there, dry. Yet, more than intellectual assent or an airtight logical demonstration,

Dulles was looking for "practical, living proof."[16] In a definitive and obliging way, he had found it on that autumnal day in Boston. Similar to John Henry Newman stating it in his classic *Apologia pro sua Vita*, Dulles admits "there is no further history to my religious opinions, since becoming a Catholic I arrived at my real home."[17]

Another factor that comes to mind is Platonic thought, which the nominally Presbyterian Dulles had studied extensively. Far less expounded in the *Republic* and *Phaedrus*, but forcefully asserted in the *Timaeus*, Plato sees humanity living in a world that is "the moving image of eternity."[18] The utterly transcendent God could communicate to finite realities while not altering their intrinsically contingent natures. This tallies well with the Hebrew notion of God and with the Christian concept of the incarnation of the second person of the Blessed Trinity. Christ is "the [visible] image of the invisible God" (Col 1:15), as Saint Paul teaches. Christian Platonists make abundant use of the Hebrew notion of God-Yahweh as the "I AM WHO I AM" (Exod 3:14).

When reading Thomas Aquinas's *De Veritate* in the Jesuit scholasticate of Woodstock, Maryland, he discovered this treatise was by no means a dry and remote deliberation, but contained a rich theology based on lived, personal experience.[19] Additionally, in Woodstock, he was exposed to the symbolism of Paul Tillich and the retrieval of the spirit-filled texts of the Church fathers via ressourcement theology represented by the works of Henri de Lubac, Jean Daniélou, and Yves Congar. Fittingly, when in Rome to earn his doctorate in sacred theology at the Gregorian University, he first intended to write a doctoral thesis "on the metaphor of illumination in the religious epistemology of Saint Thomas" with fellow Jesuit Bernard Lonergan.[20] Apparently, he had been intrigued by this topic as it was congenial to his own faith experience and consonant with that of Saint Paul on his way to Damascus, the position of Augustine, and the teaching of Bonaventure. Upon returning to Woodstock, he began teaching, among others, a course on revelation, using material from fellow Jesuits Vincent O'Keefe, René Latourelle, and Karl Rahner. It was his conviction that apologetics must build upon "the power of committed religious testimony."[21]

Later, while at Catholic University of America, he published *Models of Revelation* in 1983. He considers this book as the most significant and systematic of his writings.[22] In this oeuvre, he operated mostly within the same method as with his other classic, *Models of the Church*.[23] No one model can be taken exclusively as a vehicle transporting the ineffable mystery of divine self-communication. Whereas neo-Scholastic methodology would opt in favor of one single concept or image, he preferred a dialogical approach à la Socrates. Building upon the insights of *Revelation Theology: A History*,[24] he presents five models in current theology, analyzing their respective strengths and weaknesses. Thereupon, he develops his notion of "symbolic communication" as a dialectical tool. He insists that in every model one encounters some form of symbol. Dulles favors the concept of "experiential expressivism" borrowed from George Lindbeck. This permits Dulles doing justice to two seemingly independent concerns: (1) affirming his own experience of revelation in 1940; and (2) recognizing the historical and doctrinal content of revelation. Consequently, Dulles apprehends both the subjective and objective elements of revelation within the context of symbolic realism. Revelation occurs wherever God acts in history, insofar as something divine is revealed and communicated in a living community.

One of the theological *loci* of Dulles was contemporary experience. This experience becomes a theological source as it is informed by the gospel. Again, one is reminded of Dulles the student reading the gospel parables after the experience on the banks of the Charles River. This sense of balance between freedom of experience and integration into a Catholic intellectual symphony—a hallmark of Dulles's theology, did not come about by chance. Rather, it is grounded in Ignatian spirituality. Saint Ignatius enjoins his comrades to act against anything that might lead away from total fidelity to Christ and his hierarchical Church. Memorably, this is called the *agere contra* in the *Spiritual Exercises*.[25] Thereby, Cardinal Dulles was ever mindful that theology is constitutively also a spiritual effort. In his estimation, to remain faithful to the Word of God, the theologian must be willing to constantly reference his conclusions to the Church. In submitting the fruits of his labors to the living community, that is the Church, he assures that his works can be a blessing to the people of God.[26]

MODELS OF REVELATION

First published in 1983, *Models of Revelation* is one of Cardinal Dulles's more significant books. Revelation is a complex and polyvalent reality, an inexhaustible richness. No one linguistic human structure can grasp it fully. The typology of models is at times explicative, sometimes explorative.[27] Quite Platonically, the models complement one another in illuminating the one, abstract reality of revelation from concrete particularities. Systematic thought is the process of abstraction from the particular to the universal, from symbol to system. There exists a multiplicity of approaches. Each model is faithful to Scripture and Tradition. Together, they offer approximations to the phenomenon of Christianity in history.[28] The Christ-symbol integrates and perfects all models. He considers it essential to be mindful of the Holy Spirit as the enabling principle of Christian faith (see 1 Cor 12:3).[29] Along with his fellow Jesuit Pierre Rousselot (1878–1915),[30] he is convinced one could not muster the strength to make sense of faith without the grace of supernatural light. One must entrust oneself to it.[31]

The models do not enjoy equal rank. Neither can one opt only for one model, nor can one select eclectically elements from a variety of models to solve a question. Likewise, one would find it extremely difficult to harmonize models or superimpose an altogether different model. Rather, Dulles advocates a "dialectical retrieval" in *Models of Revelation*.[32] Its modus operandi, he specifies in *A Church to Believe In*, is "a community of disciples."

In a diachronic and synchronic manner, Dulles identifies five models:

Revelation as Doctrine

In this model, Scripture is perceived as containing "inspired and inerrant teachings." Understanding it as a compilation of propositional statements, this approach would imply that everyone gifted with reason must accept Christian faith as objectively true. The proper response can only be assent to such formulation. It reveals in a definitive and intelligible way the salvific works of God in the Old Testament and in Jesus Christ.[33] Evangelicals and neo-Scholastics would favor this perspective.

The Historical Model of Revelation

In this case, a seemingly diametrically opposed position is taken. Here, God makes use of the often conflicted course of human history to reveal himself. "God reveals himself primarily in his great deeds, especially in those which form the major themes of biblical history."[34] This model thematizes God's action in concrete time and space and lets God impart information about himself. Along with Hegel, one trusts that the purpose of all history is unlocked by its anticipation in Jesus Christ.[35] Oscar Cullmann, Wolfhart Pannenberg, and G. Ernest Wright are considered inspired by this model.

Revelation as Inner Revelation

This third model, emphasizing inner experience as principal access to the numinous, is decidedly subjective in nature. As "privileged interior experience of grace or communion with God," it disclaims any exterior mediation of God.[36] The divine is a matter for the individual to encounter. It brings forth a religious *habitus* as the individual lives, henceforth, from his or her response to this experience. Not dogmatic content, but the experience of God's infinite charity enjoys central attention. Theologians such as Friedrich Schleiermacher, Auguste Sabatier, and George Tyrrell belong to supporters of this approach.

Revelation as Dialectical Presence

To overcome both the seemingly impersonal doctrinal and historical models of revelation and the perceived too subjective model of interior experience after World War I, the dialectical model of revelation was advocated. In the estimation of this group of theologians, the utter transcendence of God is thereby safeguarded.[37] Exclusively by God's sovereign self-disclosure can a person recognize God's presence. Mediated by Scripture and Christian proclamation, God's self-revelation stands in dialectical tension with humankind. Suddenly in life a word stands apart, "charged with divine power."[38] Here, the divine Logos becomes the compression and intensification for all revelation. Scripture is not revelation but refers to it. Dulles states, "When the Holy Spirit is pleased to speak through the ministry of the Church, the preached word and the sacraments become the bearers of revelation."[39] The only proper responses are faith and humble obedience. Karl Barth, Rudolf Bultmann, Emil Brunner, and Gerhard Ebeling espouse this position.

Revelation as New Awareness

In this fifth and last model, revelation occurs "as an expansion of consciousness or shift of perspective when people join in the movements of secular history. God…[is] not a direct object of experience but is mysteriously present as the transcendent dimension of human engagement in creative tasks."[40] The immanence of God expresses itself in the participation of men and women who experienced his presence in their living out gifts of creativity and imagination. In Augustine's realization that God created all, including himself, he becomes a paradigm of this model for Dulles.[41] Something like an a posteriori realization is expressed: of an ongoing presence of God without ever becoming exhausted in the world. The thus revealing God is the "stimulation of the human imagination."[42] This allows human beings to give structure to experience and to the transformation of the world. With diverse accentuations and interpretations, Dulles considered Maurice Blondel, Paul Tillich, Karl Rahner, Gregory Baum, Gabriel Moran, David Tracy, and Adolf Darlap as subscribing to this view. Also, Gustavo Gutiérrez and Leonardo Boff write under the influence of this model.

Dulles stresses that these five models are not an exhaustive description of the reality of revelation. Despite their openness, among these something Hans-Georg Gadamer called "a fusion of horizons" seems also to occur. Attended by indirectly represented features, the at-first-unthematized field of reality reveals in this process the divine as a whole.[43] Here, Dulles seeks a unifying notion or concept that can capture all five of these models without weakening any of their respective strengths.

There are, for Dulles, two realities that unite the five models of revelation into one reality with different moments: Jesus Christ and the concept of symbol. Quoting *Gaudium et Spes* 22: "Only in the mystery of the incarnate Word does the mystery of man take on light," he apprehends Jesus Christ as the God-man (1) revealing true humanity to humankind and (2) enabling access to God's self-communication.[44] Significantly, he observes, "Only in a spiritual movement toward finite realities can one actuate the sense of the transcendent as that which goes beyond the world."[45]

SYMBOLIC MEDIATION

The poets have long been familiar with the connection between symbol and revelation. Samuel Taylor Coleridge affirmed very simply, "It is by Symbols alone that we can acquire intellectual knowledge of the Divine."[46]

Defining *Symbol*

A "symbol" in Greek antiquity and in Christianity is something calling for other parts to join it to form a unity. A symbol calls for a complementary other half. Two friends use the two broken halves of a ceramic piece to recognize each other after years of separation in Greek antiquity.[47] For Plato, human existence is essentially symbolic. Transcending the androgyne myth, "each of us is accordingly only the σύηβολον (i.e., symbol or half) of a human being, because we have been cut, like flat-fish, out of a pair. Each of us is always looking for the σύηβολον that belongs to him."[48] For Christians, the *sym-bolum*, or creed, is indispensable to facilitating a common profession of faith. The *synballein*, the endless "falling or fitting together" of human beings and of reality, grants awareness of the presence of the divine. Thus, human beings go beyond themselves and reach out toward the ineffable.[49]

Influenced largely by the theology of Karl Rahner,[50] the religious studies of Mircea Eliade,[51] and the philosophy of Michael Polanyi, Dulles presents his own understanding of symbol as an integration of the five models of revelation. A symbol is a sign with an almost inexhaustible "plenitude of meaning."[52] Revelation is by its very nature symbolic. Symbol and symbolism possess four distinct qualities: (1) they offer "participatory knowledge," (2) they effect "transformation" in the human being, (3) they influence human "commitments, behavior, and actions," and (4) they enable "new avenues of awareness" and insight.[53] A symbol may thus be experienced by a human being as a personal gift compelling him to be involved in the represented. The polyvalent dynamics of symbol and symbolism touch and involve the knower as a person to such a degree that they transform him. As this experience is considered as resulting from grace, a correlation of symbol, revelation, and grace occurs. Importantly, he states, "What is immediate, for Rahner, is the self-communication of the divine, the experience of grace. But the inner presence of God cannot be known and cannot achieve itself except insofar as it becomes mediated, or mediates itself, in created symbols."[54]

Fully *d'accord* with Aristotle's famous definition of the human being as *zoon noetikon*, Dulles contextualizes the symbolic structure of reality in society. Self and reality are known through language, and language is eminently symbolic. As Rahner observes, "The symbol strictly speaking (symbolic reality) is the self-realization of a being in the other, which is constitutive of its essence."[55] The polarity of the self and the other is dovetailed by the polarity of body and spirit.[56]

A symbol is assigned cognitive value beyond that of propositional truths. Michael Polanyi's[57] studies on human knowledge have informed significantly Dulles's teaching of symbolic mediation and thereby of revelation as well. Dulles acknowledges, "A glimmer of light came to me when I was able to see, with Polanyi's help, the distinction between tacit and explicit knowing."[58] It elevated the notion of Plato that there is no exhaustive understanding of reality, which Saint Thomas recognized *quaedam cognitio obumbrata et obscurata admixta*[59] as a language communicable to a scientific age. Truth can exist for the critical human mind even if it is not stated in propositional or formal terms. No matter what is known, it remains veiled as the gulf between sender and recipient, between the absolute and contingent remains. The content of revelation is thus revealing the veiledness of the author. "If God were to communicate by signs with clearly defined meanings, He could not tell us more than we could conceive and express within the categories derived from our day-to-day experience of the world."[60] Dulles highlights *Dei Filius*, the Vatican I Dogmatic Constitution on Faith, as it confirms this salient feature of the symbolic self-disclosure of the divine: "Divine mysteries of their very nature so excel the created intellect that even when they have been given in revelation and accepted in faith, that very faith keeps them veiled in a sort of obscurity, as long as 'we are exiled from the Lord' in this mortal life, 'for we walk by faith and not by sight' (2 Cor 5:6–7)."[61] In symbolic self-disclosure, two incommensurable realities interact but the divine remains absolute and the contingent remains relative.

John Henry Newman, the British convert and fellow cardinal-theologian was another thinker who significantly informed Dulles. In his celebrated and seminal work *An Essay in Aid of a Grammar of Assent*, he demonstrates the legitimacy of apprehension without prior understanding.[62] In his estimation, apprehension is an intelligent acceptance of an idea or fact that an unexamined proposition enunciates. In the second part of his book, Newman shows the illative sense as a mental faculty filling the gap in concrete situations that require speedy action. Often, a propositional inference could never achieve this, or it could never attain logical certainty at all. In such conditions, the illative sense allows certitude.

The Nature of Symbolism

Symbolic epistemology is foundational for revelation and cannot be divorced from everyday life.[63] Dulles's employing the notion of symbolic mediation to describe the process of revelation demonstrates that symbolism is not extraneous to Christian faith, as revelation "is always mediated through symbol."[64]

This is borne out in the two kinds of knowledge human beings have: "objective knowledge" and "participatory knowledge."[65] Often knowledge is derived by dwelling in the community: one also dwells in the symbol, both using and relying on it.[66] Within the symbolic context, language, word, and gesture allow one to go beyond the prima facie value of something. Dulles reminds the reader that the Hebrew term for *word*, *dabar*, like its Greek cognates *logos* and *rhema*, when connected to God, is far broader than the mere lexical entry. It becomes synonymous with divine revelation.[67] It enables "participatory awareness" by living the communal quest for God, worshipping and believing in him. Such ecclesially grounded faith is one of an active relationship of love, described as "living in," "attending from," "dwelling in," and "participating in."[68] Such a life is not static but leads to conversion and transformation. "If revelation came simply as abstract propositional truth or historical information, the act of faith by which it was accepted could be a merely theoretical assent. But if revelation is symbolic truth, the act by which it is accepted must express itself in conduct."[69] Such symbolic realism does not, however, reduce revelation to symbol: "there must be at least a formal distinction between the symbol and what it points to." To substantiate his point, Dulles refers to the Chalcedonian definition of the two natures of Jesus Christ and its appropriation in Vatican II's *Lumen Gentium*,[70] which claims the human and divine natures in the divine Logos, Christ, form but a "single interlocked reality."[71]

Dulles differentiates three typologies of symbolism:

1. "Cosmic or nature symbolism" makes use of physical phenomena to lead the beholder beyond the merely tangible and concrete.

2. "Historical symbolism" is a category that refers to something tangible in history, but beyond the actual experience of the subject. A case in point is the cross. For Christians, it refers to a concrete historical event two thousand years ago, but through the historical symbol, immediate contact can be established.

3. "Sacramental symbolism" refers to the worship, ritual, and sacramental life of the Church. Here, "revelation is not merely knowledge about God; it is the very being of God, symbolically bestowed."[72] It can impart the very essence of God. While tangible, social, and historic, symbols are also true revealers of the numinous.[73]

For Dulles, there is certitude in revelatory symbolism.[74] Rahner and others speak "paradoxically of 'mediated immediacy.' This term aptly conveys the dualism of the explicit and the implicit, the thematic and the unthematic, the datum and the horizon in any revelatory experience. What is immediate, for Rahner, is the self-communication of the divine, the experience of grace. But the inner presence of God cannot be known and cannot achieve itself except insofar as it becomes mediated, or mediates itself, in created symbols. The symbols, however, do arouse a genuine awareness of the divine itself—an awareness that always surpasses all that we can say about it."[75]

This certitude of not falling victim to a hysteria or a psychic sickness but sharing in divine self-disclosure is to be gained through the (sacramental-ecclesial) indwelling, that is, "the personal participation of the knower in what he knows," as Polanyi is quoted by Dulles.[76] As the Jesuit theologian elaborates,

> The new identity is one that each Christian shares with others. It is the corporate identity of the Christian community, into which the individual is integrated as an extension of his or her own self. Christians see and hear no longer with their own eyes and ears alone, but with those of the Church to which they now belong. They think its thoughts, and it thinks in them. Their faith is a participation in the faith of the Church, to which they submit as the rule of their own believing. They know what the community knows, not with mere spectator knowledge, whereby one gazes at something, but by an inner familiarity, through indwelling, somewhat as we know our own bodies.[77]

This inner familiarity or validation he calls the *sensus fidelium*, or "the sense of the faithful." In this reality, communal knowledge is acquired through an immersion in revelatory tradition. This is what Dulles equates for the individual with the "illative sense" of John Henry Newman. It is acquired with inner certitude in the community of faith. For Dulles, the scientist Polanyi's concepts of "indwelling" and "tacit knowledge" and the theologian Newman's notions of "implicit reasoning" and "illative sense" meet.[78] The criteria for verifying a (theory of) revelation are (1) faithfulness to Scripture and Christian Tradition, (2) internal coherence,

(3) plausibility, (4) adequacy to experience, (5) practical faithfulness, (6) theoretical fruitfulness, and (7) value for dialogue.[79]

Upon this background, the symbolic whole of God's self-disclosure in Jesus Christ becomes comprehensible. Dulles's defining Jesus Christ as a "'presentative symbol' corresponds approximately to what Karl Rahner has called 'symbolic reality' (*Realsymbol*) as distinct from 'symbolic representation' (*Vertretungssymbol*)."[80] In this vein, *Dei Verbum*, precisely by avoiding "the impression that the church already possesses a total grasp of revelation in its fullness," conveys a dynamic understanding of revelation.[81] "The fullness of revelation is not a vocal or written word, but Christ himself, who 'is both the Mediator and at the same time the fullness of all revelation.'"[82] As a sacramental community grounded in the Eucharist, the Church is obliged to adhere faithfully to "'the mystery of the Lord,' the 'Christian dispensation,' the 'new and definitive covenant.'"[83] The ecclesial community, that is, primarily the Catholic Church as "bearer of revelation," is the indispensable locus for a fuller grasp of God's self-disclosure without ever being able to fully define it.

THE CHURCH AS BEARER OF REVELATION AND CAUSE FOR TRANSFORMATION

Dulles defines the Church as a community of disciples of Jesus Christ.[84] The Church was born by the Word of God. Thus, it conserves the Word, does not cease to meditate it, to repeat it, and to bring it to reflection in human beings of all ages and places. As the "complex reality" (*LG* 8), the Church is the self-manifestation of divine revelation. To present this reality better, Dulles borrows from George Lindbeck's "cultural-linguistic" approach.[85] In the Church, two significant processes occur simultaneously: "socialization" and "traditioning." By "traditioning," Dulles means something akin to a dialogue of worship, Scripture, the writings of the Church fathers, the teaching office, and the sense of the faithful.[86] Thereby, "reexpression and resymbolization" occur. In the ecclesial society, the formation of its members occurs within the ever-deeper articulation of faith. An atmosphere of personal trust leads to a transformation through revelation. Comprehension of knowledge occurs only via experiencing, expressing, and acting it. "The church and its members know the God of Jesus Christ by a kind of personal familiarity, by dwelling in the faith. Faith-knowledge is, in the first instance, tacit. It is a kind of instinct or second nature that prompts us to worship and to behave as believers do."[87] The believers become aware of a deeper presence of the divinely transcendent. The process is a guided one. "The Holy Spirit, animating the church, produces in faithful members an instinctive sense of what agrees or disagrees with revelation."[88] In line with Karl Rahner's thinking, Dulles views doctrines and creeds as solidifying dimensions of revelation itself. Symbols enable the cognitive dimension of revelation and doctrine as more, not less than "an objectivist form of knowledge" to be maintained. "While verbal formulations are not revelation they are necessary within the ecclesial context 'in order that man may realize himself in his humanity as a believer and achieve solidarity with his fellow believers.'"[89] This allows Dulles to conclude, "Scripture, tradition and the magisterium are inseparable and mutually interdependent (*DV* 10). Since the three are reciprocally coinherent, no one of them can be used as a totally independent source to judge or validate the other two."[90] It is important for Dulles to maintain that tradition "is the church's continuing capacity to interpret, to discern [and] to penetrate" the "tacitly known." Far from retrograde, tradition is the cause for development and expansion.[91] Tradition is the result of a real, living self-communication of God.

TRADITION AS THE INNER MOMENT
OF REVELATION

For Dulles, "tradition involves a communal 'sense of the faith.'" It is the ecclesial community that vouches and offers ever again "access to the tradition." By indwelling in revealed faith in the forms of ritual, liturgical, and moral participation, the believer experiences the implicit normative dimensions of faith. "Although tradition necessarily includes a tacit component, it has to some degree found normative expression in the writings of the fathers, in liturgical texts, and in other ecclesially certified 'monuments of tradition.'"[92] This leads him to perceive in tradition something offering continuity and identity. Aroused by a living God, tradition is "divine," "apostolic," and "living." It is held in "equal dignity" as Scripture. In contrast to a closed canon of Scripture, divine tradition enables a variety of human traditions. Dulles reminds the reader that "symbols are not infinitely malleable." Therefore, he suggests "human traditions, while needed to make divine tradition concrete and tangible, must constantly be scrutinized for their soundness and relevance." The teaching office is the "authoritative judge" regarding the conformity of particular positions with the word of God.[93] It protects the particularity of the Christian revelation from collapsing into a Hegelian chapter of human self-realization.[94]

CONCLUSION

Athanasius observes in the fourth century, "He, indeed, assumed humanity that we might become God. He manifested Himself by means of a body in order that we might perceive the mind of the unseen Father."[95] Thomas Aquinas states unequivocally, *Sacra doctrina est scientia* (sacred doctrine is knowledge) in the thirteenth century.[96] And defining to no small degree the course of modern theology, Schleiermacher does not take up the challenge to confront Kant head-on with a Christian understanding of revelation, but has Christian revelation lost its uniqueness when he writes, "What is revelation? Every original and new intuition of the universe is one."[97] Consistent with this reinterpretation of revelation, Paul Tillich hinges revelation on the "inner experience." "There are no revealed doctrines, but there are revelatory events."[98] Has Dulles overcome the infelicitous reception of Kantian transcendental idealism? He has convincingly contributed to it. Cardinal Dulles's elucidations on the Catholic understanding of revelation are intelligible, natural, and defensible.

In his diachronic reflections on the multifaceted nature of revelation, Cardinal Dulles demonstrates his analytic gifts and synthetic powers as a systematic theologian. His introduction of symbolism never yields to the temptation of an eclectic understanding of God's self-disclosure.

Appropriating the nineteenth-century theologian John Henry Newman's understanding of the *sensus fidelium*, he states that the Church is over time and space, along with Scripture and Tradition, the vehicle and interpreter for revelation. It is consonant with Vatican II's definition of the *Church* as "communion." Yet Dulles cautions the reader that "we have not tried to construct a full theology of revelation."[99] No sociocultural paradigm can exhaust the experience of the ineffable.

By defining *revelation* "as a complex reality consisting of the inspired word as 'the formal element and the historical event as the material element,'"[100] Dulles was able to overcome a fixation exclusively on the propositional model of revelation, while maintaining the coherence, definitiveness, and intelligibility of Catholic doctrine. Reminding one of Lonergan,[101] he rejects as false the alternative between objective and subjective and insists there can be no objectivity without subjectivity. He refers to the "striking advantages" in view of "practical fruitfulness for unity and growth of the church," for its faithfulness to early Christianity and for fostering "a lively sense of mission."[102]

Affirming Cardinal Dulles's own conversion experience, Polanyi had informed him of a subsidiary awareness, inconstruable by reason alone, but accountable to reason.[103] Inspired by Dulles, Gerald O'Collins wrote on models of resurrection.[104] For Dulles, the task of Christian faith is to enable a relationship between man and God, which finds in Christian symbols a preferred tool. Along with Rahner, he apprehends in Jesus Christ the *Realsymbol* of the mystery of God, the true historic visibility of the self-expression of God in history. Jesus, in offering everyone his disposition, allows people to communicate in the power of the Holy Spirit and to enter into communion with God.[105]

As Dulles observes, "Revelation, rather than being presupposed as fully known from the start, is progressively elucidated as theology carries out its task. As the joint meaning of all the clues and symbols whereby God communicates himself, revelation is the source and center, the beginning and the end, of the theological enterprise."[106]

5

BIBLICAL APOLOGETICS

Edward T. Oakes, SJ

As America's most distinguished theologian, Avery Cardinal Dulles made peerless contributions to theology in numerous fields: ecclesiology, revelation, dogmatics, ecumenism, interreligious dialogue, and apologetics, among others—all with his characteristic lucidity. It will be the task of future generations to discover in which of these fields his contributions will prove most significant. While not claiming, at this early stage, that *apologetics* will be judged his most signal contribution to theology, we will discuss here why his achievements in this field have been—and hopefully will continue to be—so important for the life of the Church.

Perhaps Father Dulles's contributions to apologetics will prove to be the *least* significant part of his legacy, not because of its lesser value vis-à-vis dogmatics or ecclesiology, or still less because his own work in the field is insignificant. No, the problem is the nature of apologetics itself, which is the most ephemeral and time bound of all the theological disciplines, the one least likely to last to the next generation:

> Each generation uncovers new evidence and proposes new questions. The Christian apologist must try to master all the principal arguments of credibility within the reach of his own age and to meet, so far as he can, the difficulties and anxieties of his own contemporaries.[1]

Inevitably, this challenge to meet contemporary objections will mean that the task of apologetics never ends; and what satisfies one age will prove inadequate in a new era of history. The Church certainly was up to these various challenges through the ages. But in many ways, the task nowadays is even more daunting: secularism, atheism, Darwinism, the challenge of a resurgent Islam, the mind-body problem, theodicy (itself, in certain respects, a subdivision of apologetics)—all these challenges are set before the Christian apologist. In this chapter, however, we will focus on one issue—the historical criticism of the Bible—where the cardinal's contributions will prove of value not just for our own times but also for later generations, and that, in itself, is a remarkable feat in the history of apologetics.

THE CHALLENGE OF BIBLICAL CRITICISM

Because the Bible is what it is, because its canon is fixed and will always remain so, and because it speaks throughout of certain historical events as themselves testimonies of God's action in the world, the challenge represented by the historical-critical method will never go away. Perhaps the best way to see the nature of this challenge would be to glance, however briefly, at John Henry Newman's *Tract 85*, written during his Anglican days. This important tract was later overshadowed by his much more famous *Tract 90*, but it still speaks to us today. In that, perhaps his second-most famous tract, Newman points out, no doubt for the first time for some of his readers, the central problem that the Bible represents for the apologete: its apparent inconsistencies. For example, the two accounts of Creation in Genesis, discrepancies between Deuteronomy and Exodus in their accounts of Moses, and the two variants of the Ten Commandments. Within the New Testament, Newman noted the presence of only a single narrative of the raising of Lazarus, the different texts of the Sermon on the Mount or Plane in Matthew and Luke, accounts disagreeing about who bore the cross on the way to Calvary, discrepancies between Matthew and Acts over the death of Judas, and the distinct accounts of the resurrection and ascension.

Subsequent scholarship only compounded the problem. For example, why did Samuel express misgivings about the idea of anoint-

ing a king (see 1 Sam 8:6–8) when Deuteronomy (supposedly an earlier book and one from the pen of Moses at that) clearly called on the
people to anoint kings (see Deut 17:14–20)?[2] Or, closer to home for the
Christian, both Mark and Matthew report that Jesus miraculously
walked on water, but Mark concludes the episode with the observation
that the disciples were confused because their hearts were still blinded
(Mark 6:49–52), and Matthew adds, "Those in the boat worshiped
him, saying, 'Truly you are the Son of God'" (Matt 14:33). And so on.

None of these narrative variants in the Bible will be surprising to
even the most mildly literate believer or secularist. But the ability of the
apologist to explain the *meaning* of these discrepancies is no less exigent
for all their contemporary familiarity. We all know from the confusion
sown by *The Da Vinci Code* what can happen to the faith of the faithful
if they are not adequately forearmed with proper responses to these
discrepancies.

At first, that exigency was felt more acutely by Protestants than
Catholics, for obvious reasons. The whole rationale for raising the ban-
ner of *sola scriptura* as the methodological rubric for adjudicating all later
doctrinal disputes collapses if Scripture cannot be heard to speak in one
voice. If Scripture speaks in many voices, how can the believer reconcile these discordances without violating the principle of *sola scriptura*?
Even before the rise of historical criticism made the dilemma of
Protestant doctrine so painful, Catholic controversialists were quick to
see the dangers in the *sola scriptura* rubric.

For Catholics, only cacophony could result in the principle of *sola
scriptura* provided it remained unmoored from an ecclesiastical authority competent to pronounce on the meaning of Scripture. For a while,
Catholics seemed immune to the dilemma; but that immunity eventually proved an illusion, as *Tract 85* in effect foretold. As evidence of the
Bible's heavy debt to its environment grew in the nineteenth century—
that is, when translations of the Egyptian *Book of the Dead*, Mesopotamian
law codes, and Sumerian and Babylonian versions of *The Epic of
Gilgamesh* became available to the reading public—the Catholic Church
could no longer ignore the issue.

At first, the Church's Magisterium responded with a fierce attack
on "Modernism"; under that umbrella was included any notion that

Moses did not personally write the Pentateuch or that the Gospels were not all direct accounts of the *ipsissima verba et gesta Jesu*. But even at the height of the success of the campaign against Modernism, when seminaries largely ignored a historical-critical approach to the Bible, cracks were beginning to appear, until the Magisterium eventually took note; and, in a truly revolutionary document, Pope Pius XII asserted in *Divino Afflante Spiritu* (1943),

> What is the literal sense of a passage is not always as obvious in the speeches and writings of the ancient authors of the East, as it is in the works of our own time. For what they wished to express is not to be determined by the rules of grammar and philology alone, nor solely by the context; the interpreter must, as it were, go back wholly in spirit to those remote centuries of the East and with the aid of history, archaeology, ethnology, and other sciences, accurately determine what modes of writing, so to speak, the authors of that ancient period would be likely to use, and in fact did use.[3]

To be sure, the pope is speaking here primarily of issues pertaining to the Old Testament, but nothing in what he says above can be said to exclude a priori the New Testament either, very much including the Gospels. Once again, as *The Da Vinci Code* shows, the results of historical research into the Gospels have filtered down to the ordinary believer (and unbeliever) in the most irresponsible ways. But that is precisely the challenge of the apologete! And because matters touching on the historicity of Jesus obviously affect the Christian faith far more radically than even that appertaining to the historicity of, for example, Adam and Eve or the Exodus (touchy as those issues are), and because debate about the historical Jesus entails many technical matters, we will concentrate for the rest of this chapter on Cardinal Dulles's apologetics concerning the Gospels, focusing above all on his book *Apologetics and the Biblical Christ* and his lecture "Historical Method and the Reality of Christ."[4]

APOLOGETICS AND THE BIBLICAL CHRIST

No one can do effective apologetics without first admitting the plausibility of the objections to the Christian faith that the apologete intends to address. Quick dismissals of objections to the Christian message might be soothing for some, but they are valueless as apologetics. Celsus was not stupid, and Bertrand Russell was not an idiot. As to the challenge of historical criticism, we have already seen how Cardinal Newman began by admitting the problem, a debating strategy that one will find in all the great theologians of the Church.

One finds that spirit of serene admission of the plausibility of the opponent's viewpoint in Cardinal Dulles's portrayal of the historicity of the Gospels:

> The pure historian will treat the Gospels with great caution. He will not deny that Jesus existed or was an influential religious teacher, but he will be suspicious of precisely those details to which the Christian apologist will wish to appeal, namely, the divine claims and miracles of Jesus. On these matters the profane historical will not find the testimony of the Gospels sufficiently primitive and unbiased to upset his own postulates. He will adhere to his presumption that worldly events have natural explanations and will expunge the supernatural elements from the life of Jesus as best he can.[5]

In the face of this stark admission, the temptation on the part of the devout believer is often to panic. But such panic only arises when other presuppositions are at work, which themselves must be attacked and undermined—here, especially, the notion that it is somehow *a bad thing* that the Gospels do not meet von Ranke's standard of displaying events *wie sie eigentlich gewesen waren*, as they had "actually" happened. Quite the contrary, such a project, even if it were conceivable, which, given the ancient norms of historiography, it is not, would never convey the real Christ of the New Testament.

It is to our benefit that the Gospels were written both *ex fide* (as expressions of the personal faith of each evangelist) and *in fidem* (to bring the reader to his or her own personal faith in Christ). To want the evangelists to have done otherwise would not only be to indulge in a fool's errand but would defeat the very purpose of the documents themselves: to kindle faith in the prospective believer. The problem that apologetics faces here is that too often believers import the very skeptical norms of interpretation that make a true interpretation of the Gospels impossible. Contemporary readers of the Gospels must face this question: are they *historicists* who think only confirmed facts can be trusted, or are they *believers* who trust in the fundamental "fact" of the New Testament proclamation that "God was in Christ reconciling the world to himself"? If they are both, for Dulles they will only feel turmoil:

> At this point, the Christian historicist will experience a sense of distress. He will regret the way in which the Evangelists went about their task. A little impatiently, he will ask why they did not identify themselves and their sources more accurately. Why did they not reproduce more exactly what they found in the fonts rather than tamper with it as we have seen? Why did they not obtain and pass on to us more precise details about the words and miracles of our Lord? From this point of view, it seems regrettable that we have only the testimony of believers. Would not the Evangelists have done better to incorporate some depositions from neutral witnesses, such as medical reports of the type that the modern Church demands for canonization processes?[6]

In a word, no! "As confessional documents, the Gospels speak only to potential or actual believers," says Dulles. "They contain nothing to satisfy the imagination of the novelist or the curiosity of the chronicler. They do not present Jesus 'according to the flesh' but as seen in the light of the Spirit. Only to the man who is earnestly seeking communion with God will the Gospels yield their full message."[7]

True as this point is, it might seem at first glance to represent the abandonment of apologetics in favor of an outright kerygmatic approach: here is the good news, believe or not as you will, but a decision must be made one way or the other, quite independent of prior "rational" arguments for the faith. For is that not, after all, the approach of Saint Paul, who seems to eschew apologetics in all its forms in his own preaching?

> For the message about the cross is foolishness to those who are perishing, but to us who are being saved it is the power of God....Where is the one who is wise? Where is the scribe? Where is the debater of this age? Has not God made foolish the wisdom of the world? (1 Cor 1:18; 20–21)

Nor is this merely Paul's view, for it characterizes Jesus's own demeanor toward himself, as Cardinal Dulles saw even in his days as an undergraduate at Harvard, as he recounts in his gripping autobiography of his conversion, *A Testimonial to Grace*:

> Christ, as He appeared in the Scriptures, was not primarily a moralist. For conduct as such He cared relatively little; love and faith He cherished above measure....The moralists never seemed to rise above the obvious. Christ never paused to state the obvious. He told of things no man had seen. Nor was He merely a philosopher, another Socrates or Plotinus. They, after long inductive processes, came to tentative conclusions about the nature of God, the immortality of the soul, and the good life. Christ, Who seemed a stranger to discursive thought, spoke readily and with finality about these matters....His knowledge of spiritual matters was direct and immediate. His doctrine, higher than that of the philosophers, did not have the same source.[8]

Apologetics has always admitted that its mode of argumentation is merely provisional and not meant to replace faith but merely to show its inherent rationality, once accepted. Precisely because the theologian is already convinced of the inherent rationality of the faith (however much it also must transcend the deliverances of reason when reason is exercised independent of faith), the Christian apologist can point out the flaws in the reasoning of the skeptic. Consider the frank admission by the apologete that the Gospels are inherently confessional, which accounts for the freedom the evangelists take in transposing chronology, fashioning the words of Jesus into clusters, stressing certain titles over others, and so on. Why should the unbeliever accept the frankly confessional writings of the New Testament if his refusal to confess is precisely the point at issue? Has not the impasse here become unbridgeable?

Not according to Dulles. Note first that in reading the New Testament "one cannot fail to be struck by the absolute firmness of its religious witness. The authors never write like philosophers groping for the final answer, nor does the language of doubt ever appear in their religious testimony."[9] This point is hardly probative, as we have just seen, since one can always attribute such certainty to delusion, but that strategy becomes harder and harder to maintain when other factors are brought in, such as these:

> New Testament doctrine about Christ is utterly novel. Nothing in the Jewish tradition—the tradition in which Peter and Andrew, James and John, Stephen and Paul and Barnabas were reared—would have predisposed them to accept what they now proclaim. Before they became Christians they would have shrunk in horror at the very thought of paying divine honors to a man. How can one explain, if not through a revelation, that they now so confidently and unanimously look upon this Galilean carpenter as Lord of the universe?[10]

At some point, the improbabilities of the skeptical denial of the Christian message begin to mount, so that the deniers start to look like irrational dogmatists who won't face the plain facts before them:

> The rational inquirer must seek to give some explanation for the genesis of the extraordinary faith and the unique religious society depicted for us in the New Testament. One answer is that given by the New Testament writers themselves. On every page they proclaim that they have not invented this doctrine, but that it has come to them through revelation. Jesus Himself has imparted the saving truth through His own

words and works. If we accept that explanation, we can readily account for all the attributes we have just noted in the message and in the witness of the primitive Church. If it be false, the faith of the first Christians is an enigma.[11]

Here is the bind that marks the career of apologetics throughout the history of theology: on the one hand, it must grant the initial plausibility of the skeptical argument (indeed, sometimes it must admit the outright *truth* of the objections raised against the believer, such as evolution, the age of the earth, or in our case, discrepancies in the Bible). On the other, it must find the flaw in the argument *without subscribing to the logic that makes that argument seem initially plausible.* For example, fundamentalism would never have arisen if fundamentalists had not already (based on their upbringing in a civilization that universally holds certain assumptions as taken-for-granted norms that "everybody" knows) subscribed to the positivistic epistemology and ontology that made them panic at biblical discrepancies in the first place. Similarly, old-style apologetics, which begins by assuming that the Gospels must be historically accurate in all their particulars or else the faith will be undermined, concedes the very premise that is the starting point of the skeptical argument. But the very lack of concern with such issues *in the New Testament itself* should point the way to a better road, as is evident in this important passage:

> We have contrasted two forms of apologetics, both based on the New Testament. The first of these would proceed by scientific historical techniques according to the postulates of the historicocritical school. The other would take a larger and more human view of the biblical testimony, attending expressly to questions of value. The first approach would seek to get behind the faith of the primitive Church and to prove its reasonability from the historically ascertainable facts related in the Gospels. The other approach—which I call confessional—would exhibit concurrently the credibility of the essential facts and of their Christian interpretation. It would invite the inquirer to assent to both in one indivisible act.[12]

Cardinal Dulles points to the way taken by the New Testament itself. Fascinatingly, Matthew himself admits that the skeptic can always resort to the hypothesis that Jesus's body was stolen to account for the empty tomb (see Matt 28:11–15). Moreover, Paul openly avows that the risen Jesus appeared only to his followers, and even then, to not very many of them (see 1 Cor 15:5–7). In other words, *no nonbeliever was ever vouchsafed a vision of the risen Jesus, and this fact is theologically significant.*

Cardinal Dulles was surely right when he drew this important conclusion from the way the New Testament depicts the resurrection:

> The style in which the apostles proclaimed the resurrection was entirely consistent with the mode in which they had learned it. If their conviction had been simply imposed by the evidence of the senses, they would perhaps have been tempted to convert others by adducing evidence of the same kind. But they were well aware that their own conviction was chiefly the result of an illumination from above. They appear before their fellow Jews not as reporters of a rare phenomenon but as heralds of a revelation. In their initial preaching—as summarized, for example, in the early chapters of Acts—they do not bother to state the details of how they have become convinced. Still less do they try to prove the fact by historical evidences. Instead they speak as authoritative witnesses. They announce the dogma as something to be accepted on their word as divinely appointed heralds.[13]

To be sure, this is no knockdown argument *preventing* someone from holding that the disciples were victims of a hallucination. But as Thomas More said in *A Man for All Seasons*, "Is it *probable?*" "A profane historian," the cardinal dryly notes, "would be mistaken if he thought [the hallucination hypothesis] a neat solution, but he might be forgiven if, on his own postulates, he judged it more admissible than the hypothesis of a real resurrection."[14] But just because a skeptic cannot admit the possibility of resurrection, based on his own naturalistic grounds, that does not make his hallucinatory hypothesis any more probable. In the wise words of William Albright, who was both a devout Christian and an eminent historian,

> What we have in [the Gospels] is…a reflection of reports of eye-witnesses who were overwhelmed by the profound experiences and the extreme tension of mind and body through which they had passed. Men who see the boundary between conventional experience and the transcendental world dissolving before their very eyes are not going to distinguish clearly between things seen in the plane of nature and things seen in the world of spirit. To speak of the latter as "hallucinations" is quite misleading, since nothing like them is otherwise known either to historians or to psychologists. Here the historian has no right to deny what he cannot disprove. He has a perfect right to unveil clear examples of charlatanry, of credulity, of folklore, but in the presence of authentic mysteries his duty is to stop and not attempt to cross the threshold into a world where he has no right of citizenship.[15]

Bearing all these often complex factors in mind, we can now see the contours of Cardinal Dulles's biblical apologetics. First, historicism—meaning the view both that the Bible recounts all historical events as they really happened *and* that the historical-critical method can *show* that it does—will always fail in its self-imposed task of convincing the already doubtful and skeptical. It is a method that basically (although its practitioners might not admit this in so many words) "seeks to get behind the interpretation of the primitive Church and to show that the facts themselves, objectively considered, admit of no other interpretation than that which Christian dogma proclaims."[16] This approach is not only forbidden by the Bible itself, which knows no other testimony to the events it speaks of but its own, it also misunderstands the role of apologetics in leading someone to the faith. Apologetics cannot, by the nature of its project, use *compulsory* reason, for that would dispense with the need for faith, which transcends, although it does not abolish, reason.

Second, we must realize that what at first seems to be the essential difficulty for apologetics is really its boon. For the New Testament in its entirety was written for those in search of religious truth. "The intrinsic sublimity of the message, its coherence, its adaptation to man's religious needs make it eminently worthy of consideration as a revelation from God," says the cardinal. "The novelty of the message and the conviction, unanimity, constancy, and spiritual power with which it was heralded, give us every reason to conclude that the apostles were the bearers of revelation. As men most intimately involved in the spiritual events of which they speak, they have an excellent claim to our trust."[17]

This approach might seem much less helpful than the old way of doing apologetics, with its serene use of syllogisms and fact-based argumentation. But leaving aside its own intrinsic difficulties in ignoring textual cruces, it also leaves too little room for faith. What the prospective believer needs to see is that, while accepting a message as from God demands faith, it is not a blind faith. The old apologetics was right that our faith is not a leap into the dark, but it *is*, nonetheless, a leap for all that. "It has a rational basis," says Dulles, "and part of that basis is provided by the New Testament."[18] But even more, it is an ecclesial faith that both addresses and fulfills man's deepest religious longings:

> The New Testament is not simply the expression of an ancient faith. We read it today with full consciousness that the religion born with the apostles still retains its vitality. The witness of the primitive Church is enhanced by the witness of the Church today. The arguments from history thus ultimately rejoin the arguments based on the living reality of the Church: its marvelous propagation, its stability through the centuries, and its undying fruitfulness in all good works. In the last analysis…there are not many signs of credibility, but only one: the whole Christ in His Church. In apologetics these two together, Christ and His Church, should be viewed as a single sign, just as in dogmatic theology they are seen to be two facets of a single mystery.[19]

This overview of the biblical apologetics of Cardinal Dulles comes from a set of lectures he gave in 1961 (the book itself bears a copyright of 1963 and an imprint date of 1966). In other words, all these insights were delivered well before the opening session of the Second Vatican Council, and certainly long before most Catholic theology and biblical scholarship had become so heavily influenced by the historical-critical method, which was first hammered out by Protestant scholars. Largely because Catholic clergy and laity were innocent both of the implications of biblical discrepancies *and* of the apologetic tools necessary to meet that challenge, Catholics were left flummoxed and their faith was undermined. For that reason, it is a pity that this short book of five lectures has not been more widely influential but fell out of print before the sixties had expired.

"HISTORICAL METHOD AND THE REALITY OF CHRIST"

So, what can we say of the time since these lectures were delivered? While the main body of Cardinal Dulles's work went in other directions—ecclesiology, primarily—he nonetheless kept abreast of the work of biblical scholars and dedicated a lecture to this theme in the early nineties, a treatment of which will bring these reflections to a conclusion.

While Catholic exegetes and theologians certainly made massive contributions both to studies on the historical Jesus (Raymond E. Brown and Joseph Fitzmyer, whose work Dulles always respected) and to a historically informed Christology (Edward Schillebeeckx, Hans Küng, about which Dulles was dubious, but more on doctrinal than historical grounds), the issues first noted by Cardinal Dulles in 1961 came to a new focus in 1991 with the near-simultaneous publication of John Dominic Crossan's *The Historical Jesus* and the first volume of John P. Meier's three-volume *A Marginal Jew*. Without going into Dulles's specific criticisms of these two works, his lecture on them, titled "Historical Method and the Reality of Christ," delivered on April 2, 1992,[20] shows both the continuity of his views together with certain new accents and nuances honed over the years of his study of biblical scholarship of Jesus.

As he rightly saw, no one ever takes up research into Jesus (or into any past event, for that matter) without prior philosophical/theological commitments. Especially in biblical scholarship, one's prior stance vis-à-vis the question of faith and history will prove determinative, whether one admits it or not. For the cardinal, there were basically four options in deciding how faith and history interrelate: one can either hold (1) that history and faith are incompatible, (2) that they are separate, (3) that history grounds faith, or finally (4) that faith grounds (in the sense of rightly interprets) history.

The first approach has been around for a long time. It arose from hostility to dogma and tried to substitute a purely human Jesus of history for the Christ of faith and dogma (e.g., Hermann Samuel Reimarus, David Friedrich Strauss, and Ernest Renan in the nineteenth century, and John Allegro, Rudolf Augstein, Morton Smith, Thomas Sheehan, and John Dominic Crossan in the twentieth century). For them, the entirety of Christian dogma about Christ rests on a mistake: all the titles that the New Testament applies to Jesus are wrong, since they are grounded in the antecedently impossible event of the resurrection. As Dulles points out, however, it is precisely this position that is dogmatic!

> Antidogmatic historicists are dogmatic in their own way, since they antecedently rule out the unique and the transcendent. Their approach ruptures the continuity between Jesus and the community of his followers. It does violence to the sources by expunging sayings and deeds of Jesus that are attested by what, according to the standard criteria, must be regarded as early and reliable traditions. Having reduced Jesus to the stature of a common prophet or wonder worker, this approach has difficulty in accounting for the extreme reactions of his followers and adversaries and for the rapid emergence of Christianity as a distinct religious faith.[21]

The second approach insists that historical criticism can never undermine the faith because it can never touch it. In twentieth-century Protestantism, this view was most famously advocated by Paul Tillich and Rudolf Bultmann and finds contemporary representation on the

Catholic scene in John Meier, who holds that, for example, the resurrection of Jesus can only be known by faith. He repeatedly reminds his readers (he is a Catholic priest) that he is not denying faith and revelation, only putting them in brackets. But when consistently applied, this method implies, when it does not directly assert, a discontinuity between faith and history that runs counter to what the faith has always been understood to mean, which is why Vatican II taught that Gospels, "whose historical character the Church unhesitatingly asserts, faithfully hand on what Jesus the Son of God, while living among men, really did and taught."[22]

The third approach, at least, recognizes that the Christian faith is grounded in history, but it can often veer too close to the view that history must therefore be allowed to *verify* the faith. We saw this earlier in Dulles's criticism of early Catholic historicists and can be found today in a more sophisticated form in Wolfhart Pannenberg, who holds that the historical-critical method can prove the resurrection as an event of history. Once again, does this approach leave enough room for faith? Can history really terminate in a firm intellectual commitment, "higher than the fluctuating judgments of probability"?[23] Would it not be more accurate to say that only under the attraction and illumination of divine grace does one finally see how the historical-critical method can *lead* one to see the historicity of the resurrection but cannot *compel* one to believe in the resurrection?

The fourth approach surely is the best because it conforms to the phenomenology both of the Gospels themselves as well as of the act of faith: "I hold that Christian faith," the cardinal says, "does not normally arise from, or rest on, a critical examination of the New Testament evidence concerning the Jesus of history. Rather, it comes from God's revealing word as conveyed by the testimony of the Church."[24]

In conclusion, we can all readily appreciate how indispensable the witness of Cardinal Dulles has been. If the Catholic theological guild had from the outset recognized his book *Apologetics and the Biblical Christ* for the seminal classic it is, Catholics would not be so confused about their faith as they now are. May his witness live on!

6

SHAPING CATHOLIC PRACTICAL THEOLOGY

Raymond J. Webb

Avery Cardinal Dulles's long and distinguished life as a systematic theologian focused on ecclesiology, with significant work also in the areas of revelation, faith, catholicity, apologetics, evangelization, and culture. Popularly known for his *Models of the Church*, which is sometimes misunderstood, he continued to use the methodology of models throughout his work.[1]

Cardinal Dulles was a great clarifier, organizer, and synthesizer, who sought to present the various major positions on a variety of theological issues fairly, critique the aspects that were deficient, and then, if possible, present a preferred position that drew on the best of the others. Regrettably, he did not have more time to devote to practical theology. Nevertheless, Dulles's work can help to shape an understanding of practical theology that is faithful to the discipline and authentically Catholic. I have written and spoken elsewhere of the importance of Catholic practical theology.[2] The work of Cardinal Dulles supports, strengthens, and nuances the argument, although his contribution has been mostly indirect.

Here, we use the term *practical theology* interchangeably with *pastoral theology* to define *Catholic practical theology* as the specialization in theology that brings Catholic teaching and concrete, specific situations into a properly ordered dialogue, leading to appropriate action. Besides general practical theological theory and issues, practical theology also includes subdisciplines such as religious education, pastoral care, pastoral counseling, ministry formation, theological pedagogy, church administration, and congregational studies. Some examples of issues that would engage practical theologians in a more general way are religion in the public square, the significance of place in Catholic-Muslim dialogue, considering human rights and national security, multiethnic parishes, and the Catholic identity of the Catholic college.

The limited Catholic contributions need augmentation. Catholic energies in the subdisciplines of practical theology may have shifted toward methodological and pedagogical concerns and away from the conversations connected to the theological academy, hence, the need for the continuing development of a "Catholic" practical theology. Kathleen Cahalan would prefer to talk of "Catholic approaches" to practical theology rather than "Catholic practical theology."[3] That presupposes a common understanding of the core of practical theology. The usual description of practical theology in current literature is not "generic" but Protestant, with its emphasis on Word, words, and rationality, therefore omitting fundamental Catholic aspects.

The larger society, the academy, and the Church all have a proper relationship to Catholic practical theology. I am convinced that practical theology, as a discipline, does matter. It grounds the way that Catholicism is lived out in solid principles, answerable to all the demands of any rigorous theological specialization. It keeps important specific issues in view and links them with the Catholic Tradition.

In this chapter, we will draw on Dulles's theological work to name several characteristics of Catholic theology that are essential in any version of practical theology that would want to be called Catholic. First, we will look at aspects of a proper understanding of the Catholic theological tradition according to Dulles. Then, we will briefly consider the scholarly dimension of theology and practical theology. Finally, we will examine aspects of Catholic practical theology, its service to the Church, and its description. True to its formal object, it must be in "conversation" with specific situations, related to both Church and world.

REVELATION

Revelation is at the heart of theology for Dulles. Revelation is understood in terms of symbol. It is "the self-manifestation of God through a form of communication that could be termed, at least in the broad sense, symbolic."[4] Revelation "does not suppress but presupposes and perfects the perceptual and cognitive faculties of the recipient… symbolic communication effects a profound conversion, carrying the subject across a logical gap and providing a new interpretive framework."[5] The symbolic communicates true affirmations about what is antecedently real.[6] For Dulles, Catholic theology does not exist without a dependence on revelation.[7]

Part of the Catholic understanding of theology regards the Bible. Dulles framed this perspective in *Apologetics and the Biblical Christ*: "[The Catholic] reads the Bible within the Church, according it that high authority which the Church assigns it, and understanding it in harmony with the whole Catholic community. The Catholic does not wish to find in the Scriptures any meaning other than that which the Church finds in them."[8]

A Catholic understanding of revelation also includes "Tradition." As Cardinal Dulles notes, "The acceptance of a divinely authoritative tradition is characteristically Catholic, as opposed to Protestant."[9] Dulles describes Vatican II's understanding of tradition, *pace* Maurice Blondel, as "a means whereby the church and its members can enter into a living relationship with God," "communicated through action, example, and worship," and progressive and dynamic.[10] Of course, revelation is always aided by reason, as we will discuss briefly later.

SACRAMENTAL

Avery Dulles points to Richard McBrien's highlighting of three theological foci of Catholicism: sacramentality, mediation, and communion:

By the principle of sacramentality, [McBrien] means the acceptance of tangible and finite realities as actual or potential carriers of the divine presence. The principle of mediation is a corollary of that of sacramentality. The universe of grace, for the Catholic, is mediated by Christ, the Church, and other signs and instruments. Communion is a further corollary. The mediation of the divine occurs in and through a community, which is in turn strengthened by the encounter; "there is no relationship with God, however intense, profound, and unique, that dispenses entirely with the communal context of *every* human relationship with God."[11]

For Dulles and McBrien, Catholicism embraces "both/and," rather than "either/or."[12] To the Protestant principle of not blurring God and creature, Dulles adds his version of the Catholic principle, which does not "banish God from his creation." There is visible mediation. Dulles highlights a sentence from the Final Report of the 1985 Extraordinary Synod of Bishops: "The Church as communion is the sacrament for the salvation of the world."[13]

Catholic practice is rooted in a general sacramental, mediational vision, as well as in the seven privileged sacraments. Certainly, Catholics share baptism with all Christians and the importance of Eucharist with many. But for Catholics, the practice of the Christian life is involved with participation in the sacraments, frequent Eucharist being at the heart of this life.

ECCLESIAL

Cardinal Dulles's models of the Church are remarkably well known and are popularly attached to his name. Some falsely interpret the models as equally desirable and useful. In fact, the models were carefully drawn positions out of which Dulles later would attempt to construct an additional model, which for him best represented the reality in question. Hence, the Communion of Disciples was not one of the original five models of the Church and was added to the second edition of the book, although described earlier in *A Church to Believe In*.[14]

Dulles's explorations of ecclesiology led him to commend the greater involvement of laymen and women in the "faith and life of the Church," in theology, and in the "ministries of teaching, music, social action, counseling, and even the distribution of Holy Communion....It is urgent that lay persons assume greater responsibility than ever for the faith and life of the church."[15] Can the laity be called ministers? Can the laity "do ministry?" Dulles's answer to both is a clear yes.[16] His staunch support of this position with theological warrants resulted in helpful guidelines for a formal relationship between the Church and laypersons officially called by the Church to engage in its work.

Note that a significant part of Cardinal Dulles's own theological work has been a response to needs of the Church. So, it seems consistent to say that part of the work of Catholic practical theology will continue in that direction. Evangelization and apologetics are important, if underdeveloped, subdisciplines of practical theology.

ECUMENICAL

Avery Dulles's work has been pioneering in the area of ecumenism. His dissertation, completed before the Second Vatican Council, was on the topic of "the participation of Protestant churches in the prophetic office of the one Church of Christ."[17] Dulles notes the Council's "reverence for the heritage of other Christian churches," "their salvific importance for their members," and "that they possess true elements of the Church of Christ."[18] His ongoing dialogue with Yale's George Lindbeck is important, even as he would take issue with Lindbeck's cultural linguistic theological perspective, which describes theological perspectives as languages in which particular believing communities come to their own religious understanding of ultimate mystery.[19] Much as he would insist on Catholic particularity, Dulles wanted a broader language, despite the difficulties associated with it.

The ecumenical partnership is also important in practical theology. Protestant scholars and practitioners have advanced the study of practical theology over the past fifty years. Catholics must draw on the work of Protestants in Europe and the United States in the development of specific areas of subdisciplines in practical theology as well as in overall theory. Catholics owe them a debt. Don Browning, Richard Osmer, Elaine Graham, Friedrich Schweitzer, Paul Ballard, Duncan Forrester, and many others enrich the disciplines.

The Protestant focus is on the biblical word and rationality as being primary. This leads Protestant practical theological discourse to be "word-centered." The increasing discourse on "practices" does not, in the long run, describe the same thing as the place of the sacraments and the sacramental sensibility in the belief and worship of Catholics.[20] The "Protestant Principle" maintains a wariness of mediation and of conflating God with creation.[21]

The Catholic partners in practical theology must assert their own sensibilities, even at the risk of challenging the conversation to expand its discourse and causing a certain discord for a time. A Catholic conceptual framework, with its living language and perspective, must be the ethos of Catholic practical theology. "Communion" ecclesiology, sacramental perspectives, the mysterious presence of grace, and the specter of sin will be important in the work of the Catholic practical theologian. One looks for hints of God and depth of meaning in life situations and in the interplay between reflection on the present and reflection from the past that is kept alive in the religious community. Appropriate action is always taken.

SCHOLARLY

In his monumental work on faith, *The Assurance of Things Hoped For*, Dulles describes faith as, *inter alia*, cognitive, reasonable, and critical. Practical theology, as one specialization of theology, of "faith seeking understanding," must be scientific, reasoned, and intellectual. As scientific, it must embrace a wide-ranging scholarly conversation that is "related to other theoretical work, connected to the literature, attentive to the perspectives of particular theologians to support, challenge, or nuance their views, engaged in the development of principles, rooted in the perspective of one school as opposed to another, set out for or against other perspectives, and contributory to theory."[22] It can be "critical" without doubting all or only favoring a hermeneutic of suspicion. Dulles insisted on the importance of philosophy in relationship to theology and to interpretation of specific situations.[23]

Some of this can be illuminated by looking at Dulles's discussion of "seminary theology and university theology." He finds the university setting more inviting to serious theological research, while the seminary will be a place of imparting teaching and theology, which is not questioned. Preaching, counseling, and sacramental ministry are important in the seminary, according to Dulles.[24] University theology is in close contact with history, literary criticism, sociology, psychology, and philosophy. It reasons critically, addresses diverse audiences, and deals with open questions.[25]

Dulles cautions that university theology can become detached from the Church and from pastoral concerns.[26] He insists that theology "requires a living relationship to a community of faith and to the official leadership of that community."[27] Dulles expects "university theology" to be in contact with the Church. This is not to say that there cannot be strong disputes and questions of interpretation and proper roles in the conversation; legitimate dissent is not precluded. But theology adrift cannot really be theology. It becomes scholarly work in the study, history, and interpretation of religion. At some point, however, one would cease to have theology, at least as understood in the "Catholic" sense described earlier.

Cardinal Dulles saw great benefit from theological interaction with the natural and human sciences, a vital and stimulating exchange between faith and reason.[28] He adapted John Henry Newman's four conditions for scientific investigation to the study of theology. It must not contradict dogma. Science must not disagree with the magisterium on theological issues. It must put forth serious positions, not seeming contradictions. It must not popularly present unsettling positions.[29] Certainly, these principles would apply to the interplay between human science and Catholic practical theology.

PRACTICAL THEOLOGY

Theology, for Dulles, is methodical reflection on the Christian faith, "concerned at every point with communication."[30] In *The Craft of*

Theology, he notes that practical theology, in which he includes apologetics, missiology, and pastoral theology, is a branch of theology in which "the role of communication has long been recognized."[31] Pastoral theology "has to do with the spiritual care of the Church's own members."[32] Apologetics, for Dulles, is concerned with promotion of the Christian message. Missiology involves "disseminating" the message where it has not been firmly planted.[33] Seemingly from an "applied theology" perspective, Dulles had earlier included moral and spiritual theology within pastoral theology, which "investigates, methodically and critically, what imperatives for Christian action arise from Christian faith."[34] Even without any extensive treatment of practical theology, Dulles's writings offer a definite character to a description of Catholic practical theology.

Significant to practical theology are the specific—unique or generic—situations with which the Tradition is connected. The notion of "applied theology" has given way to a certain "theological reflection," usually viewed as a critical two-way conversation between the Tradition and situations. Dulles asserted that one cannot require praxis to be put ahead of theory, nor "play off" the pastoral against the doctrinal.[35] Situations do raise questions calling for new reflections in light of the Tradition. Dulles had a certain wariness of subjective "experience," since it is shaped by the presuppositions one brings to it. "It can be a theological source, but only if the experience itself is informed by the gospel."[36] Dulles notes that philosophy does "make inferences from things known by common human experience...[and] the findings of philosophy and theology must agree in the end."[37] Secular culture can distort; subjectivist views or symbols can lead away from solidarity with the Catholic tradition. However, Dulles was fully aware that every day there are new, sometimes unique situations, new questions from science, technology, and everyday life, that have no assured answers. He does call for understanding in facing the deepest problems of the day.[38]

Dulles notes an "anthropological shift" in Church documents and "a much more empirical methodology, which includes a careful phenomenology of the present situation, beginning with *Gaudium et Spes*, and continuing in Paul VI's *Octogesima adveniens* and the 1971 synodal document, *Justice in the World*."[39] In specific matters, Dulles looks to the construction of "a viable theology of religious pluralism—one that gives due value to all religions without compromising the dogmatic truths of our Christian faith."[40] Aspects of interreligious dialogue and addressing the problems of the day are important considerations for practical theology. Practical theology must avoid ahistoricism on either side of the conversation. One cannot deny development and interpretation as significant in theological realization. Similarly, the histories of the persons providing descriptions and interpretations affect what is offered for dialogue, and each situation has a history and culture. As Dulles notes, "Some responsible input should be offered by the theologians of the region from which the questions come."[41] It seems that, if the Catholic Tradition is taken as normative rather than experience or concrete events and circumstances being the norm, then difficulties of improperly privileging experience or subjectivity are avoided. Indeed, practical theology's mission is to always be in contact with the specific, lest the concrete situations of life be neglected for headier realms.

IN SERVICE OF THE CHURCH

Part of practical theology's mission is to be in service of the Church. Dulles takes a strong position: "If [theology] detaches itself from the Church and makes itself accountable to some other public, such as the state or the academy, it denatures itself as theology."[42] In his brief description of practical theology, Cardinal Dulles mentions missiology and apologetics as areas of focus for practical theology. He has written extensively on apologetics, publishing *A History of Apologetics*, as well as numerous articles.[43] Certainly, practical theology is recognized as including religious education as a subdiscipline, of which evangelization, a dimension of missiology, and apologetics can be considered a part. Dulles described evangelization as "gathering new members for the Church, [as well as] the Christian education of the faithful, and the transformation of society into the likeness of God's kingdom."[44] Dulles endorses the six models or types (or dimensions or styles) of evangelization, drawn from the encyclicals of Paul VI and John Paul II, and described by doctoral student Father Timothy Byerley.[45] *Personal witness* is the example of a life dedicated to Christ. *Verbal testimony* is seen in initial proclamation, catechesis, and apologetics. *Christian worship* is directed by the believing community primarily to God. *Community* manifests love and support that makes people want to become part. *Inculturation* makes the gospel intelligible and familiar to those being evangelized in their own cultural forms. *Works of charity* is the sixth model and includes the social apostolate as well as the promotion and preservation of life. These models combine to guide the development of programs of evangelization.

MODELS FOR CLARITY

Cardinal Dulles used various lists for clarity throughout his work. The presentation of a set of models in a specific area is a clarifying list. "A model is a typology…a schematic construction that enables one to make statements potentially applicable to an indefinite number of individuals."[46] Models have some affinity with methods or schools or ways of doing and seeing. Clearly, an intellectual exercise, each model describes a significant position, together with its proponents, recognizing that there are differences between the individuals listed with any specific model and aware that combinations admit the danger of stereotyping. The positions can be subjected to vigorous critique, hopefully leading to emergent points of view that draw on the best found in the models.

This methodology developed as Dulles was considering the Church. He realized that the Church is a mystery that could not be completely captured. Various images and metaphors contain aspects of the reality. Dulles wanted to make the unspoken assumption of each point of view clear, show the strengths and weaknesses of each, and promote dialogue. Choices had to be made and certain opinions rejected.[47] Dulles used models throughout his professional life as a means of explaining different ways of addressing the same reality. Dulles would consider his *Models of Revelation* as among his finest works, promoting serious scholarly exchange and forming a platform for his discourse on symbolic realism and symbolism as at the heart of revelation and, indeed, of all of theology.[48]

The methodology of models can offer clarity in sorting the various approaches to practical theology. Without the careful elaboration that Cardinal Dulles would have brought to work on models of Catholic practical theology, let us attempt a sketch of nine:

1. *The Pastor's Theology Model* is a description of how the priest might best do his ministry, including administering the sacraments and hearing confessions. Others doing ministry in the Church would follow in his footsteps, insofar as they were authorized.

2. *The Pastoral Skills Model* teaches ministers what to recognize and do in specific situations; it may use faith sharing and a form of theological reflection at times; it does not elaborate theory at length.

3. *The Applied Theology Model* treats more traditional areas such as systematic theology, Bible, and history as areas to be learned and then brought to situations. The specific is not a partner in the discussion and does not bring its own questions to a dialogue.

4. *The Critical Correlational Model* brings questions and answers from the Tradition to questions and answers from the specific in a dialogue of equals. Experience and aspects of culture and human science are important.

5. *The Proclamation Model* speaks to the world in its own language and invites and urges the world to be converted and embrace this perspective of thought and belief. In other words, theology is the specific language of a particular faith group.

6. *The Empirical Theology Model* does thorough social scientific data gathering and analysis and interprets what is found, frequently using religious and other meaning categories.

7. *The Experiential Model* looks in depth into human experience and finds meaning and hints of God there and constructs a larger theology. Some proponents argue for a common religious core at the heart of all humanity and world religions. Work following the Empirical and the Experiential Models can appear at times to be

very similar to that found in the sociology of religion, the psychology of religion, or the philosophy of religion.

8. *The Contextual Theology Model* considers the different circumstances in which people live, recognizes that certain voices have been neglected in the past, and builds theology appropriate for the group. It exists within the larger, universal traditions, but recognizes the particular as the language of the specific believers.

9. *The Praxis Model* privileges a specific perspective on the dialogue between Tradition and situations. Exemplars are liberation theology, political theology, and feminist theology.[49]

There is a certain unfairness in such sketched models. For this reason, specific names in connection with any model have not been used. In brief comments, Cardinal Dulles noted that there is room for critical correlation as well as an additional model, an "epiphanic" model (here called Proclamation), which interprets and even transforms experience in the light of determinate revelation.[50]

May I attempt a tenth model, drawing on aspects of the other nine? A *Catholic Dialogical Model* of practical theology would attempt "thick" descriptions of situations with their particular voices and contexts; would draw on other disciplines to help in the understanding of situations; would privilege Tradition as normative but insist on a dialogue with the specific; would respect the sensitivities of Catholic notions of Word, sacraments, sacramentality, and ecclesial connection; would insist on the intellectual rigor required of scholarly work; and would be directed to appropriate action.

How might this model address, for example, the identity of the Catholic college? In practice, work using the Catholic Dialogical Model would probably lead to suggesting a Catholic college to be distinctively Catholic in values and practices, while welcoming those who are not Catholic. It would support freedom of inquiry in the research of its theology faculty while accurately presenting Catholicism in all its richness and diversity in its Catholic theology courses. It would welcome debate but not institutionalize anti-Catholic practice. This would mean providing a place for Muslim worship but not allowing embryonic stem cell research in its laboratories. If the Catholic college dealt with ministry formation, the teaching of pastoral care of Catholics in hospitals would involve accurate listening, pastoral sensitivity, and ministerial self-awareness, as well as proper understanding of the place of the sacraments in the care that occurs in hospitals. Such a Catholic college would also teach appropriate pastoral care of Lutherans and Muslims in its fullness.

CONCLUSION

We have discussed aspects of the discipline of practical theology as seen from a Catholic perspective, considering the general themes and specifics of the writings of Avery Dulles. We have argued that Catholic practical theology must be immersed in revelation, sacramental, ecclesial, ecumenical, and scholarly. The use of models assists in the analysis of the field of practical theology. Part of practical theology's work is to be in service of the Church. In the present day, this service can be importantly rendered in the areas of evangelization and apologetics. In sum, if we take the principal themes of the theological writing of Cardinal Dulles, we find that they make a significant contribution to what the shape of Catholic practical theology ought to be.

Let us conclude with the profound practical theological reflection of Cardinal Avery Dulles as he announced his retirement from Fordham University in his last McGinley Lecture on April 1, 2008:

> The most important thing about my career, and many of yours, I feel sure, is the discovery of the pearl of great price, the treasure hidden in the field—the Lord Jesus himself....Suffering and diminishment are not the greatest of evils, but are normal ingredients in life, especially in old age. They are to be accepted as elements of a full human existence....As I become increasingly paralyzed and unable to speak, I can identify with the many paralytics and mute persons in the Gospels, grateful for the loving and skillful care I receive and for the hope of everlasting life in Christ....If the Lord now calls me to a period of weakness, I know well that his power can be made perfect in infirmity. "Blessed be the name of the Lord!"[51]

CONCLUSION

From Convert to Cardinal

Anne-Marie Kirmse, OP

On November 26, 1940, a first-year student in Harvard Law School was baptized in Saint Paul's Church in Cambridge, Massachusetts. What made this occasion especially noteworthy is that the young man was a member of a prominent family both in politics and in religion. His great grandfather was Secretary of State under President Benjamin Harrison, his great-uncle was Secretary of State under President Woodrow Wilson, and his father would become Secretary of State under President Dwight Eisenhower. His family were devout Presbyterians, and his paternal grandfather was a noted Presbyterian theologian and pastor of the early twentieth century.

On February 21, 2001, this same man, who had become an octogenarian and a Jesuit priest, knelt before Pope John Paul II to receive the red hat of a cardinal. What made this occasion especially noteworthy is that this cardinal was the first U.S.-born theologian to receive this honor who was not a bishop. What happened between those two momentous events is the topic of this chapter, the life and ministry of Avery Dulles, SJ.

A CIRCUITOUS ROUTE

Avery Dulles was born in Auburn, New York, on August 24, 1918, the third and youngest child of Janet Avery Dulles and John Foster Dulles.

As he himself described it, his journey to the Roman Catholic Church took a rather circuitous route. His early childhood was spent within the confines of his religious family environment, but his own personal beliefs began to wane when he was sent to Le Rosey, a preparatory school in Switzerland. Later, at the Choate Preparatory School in Connecticut, he was attracted to various materialistic philosophies, and, by his own admission, even dabbled with atheism.[1] After graduation from Choate, his family wanted him to attend Princeton University, his father's alma mater, but Avery's desire to study history and literature led him to Harvard College instead.

It was while an undergraduate student at Harvard that Dulles began the search that would eventually lead him to rediscover faith. Already in his freshman year, he became disenchanted with personal pleasure as the sole criterion for life's decisions. If philosophy had led him away from God, it was philosophy that would help to lead him back again. Through his college courses, he became acquainted with Plato, Aristotle, and the medieval philosophers. Their teachings provided an antidote to the materialistic philosophies that once claimed his allegiance. In the spring of his junior year, he encountered God once again as a loving, personal Being, and was able to return to prayer for the first time in many years.

Avery Dulles's search for a Church in which to nurture his reclaimed belief was a serious venture. Specializing in Italian Renaissance studies at Harvard, he realized that "at every point I found myself more at home with the Catholic tradition than with its Protestant counterparts."[2] The piety of the parishioners in the local Cambridge Catholic churches also made a deep impression on the young Dulles. Finally, his careful application of the four marks of the true Church and his assiduous research led him to desire to become a Catholic, even though at the time he did not even know how to meet with a priest. His commitment to finding the true Church was so strong that forty years later he could still say, "Catholic preachers and teachers, by and large, can be counted upon to transmit not simply their own personal opinions, but the faith of the Church. If I had not perceived this to be the case, I, for one, would not be a Catholic."[3]

With the outbreak of World War II, Dulles joined the United States Naval Reserve, serving in the Caribbean Sea and in the Mediterranean Theater of Operations. For his part in the war effort, he was decorated with the Croix de Guerre by the French Government. Shortly after his discharge in 1946, he entered the Society of Jesus (the Jesuits). He was ordained a priest in 1956 and received his doctoral degree from the Gregorian University in Rome in 1960. Afterward, he served on the faculties of Woodstock College, Fordham University, and The Catholic University of America, and was a visiting professor in colleges and universities in the United States and Europe. He retired from Catholic University in 1988 to become the Laurence J. McGinley Distinguished Professor of Religion and Society at Fordham University.

From eighty-eight years of age until his retirement in 2008, he taught at Fordham and at the Archdiocese of New York's seminary at Dunwoodie, lectured both in the United States and abroad, and served as a consultant to the Committee on Doctrine of the United States Conference of Catholic Bishops.

A FUNDAMENTAL THEOLOGIAN IN FOUNDATIONAL THEOLOGY

Dulles was a prolific writer as can be seen in his list of publications. He has published twenty-three books, with one more in press scheduled for publication later this year, and over eight hundred articles, essays, and reviews. His writings concentrate on revelation, faith, ecclesiology, and ecumenism, but are not limited to these topics. His writings have been translated into Italian, French, German, Spanish, Portuguese, Dutch, Greek, Polish, Korean, and Hungarian, and are available in digital versions and online.

The number of lectures and articles Dulles wrote each year almost staggers the imagination, and each was carefully researched and prepared. It would be an impossible task to try to present the many topics he treated during one lecture. He described himself as a fundamental theologian, that is, someone who works in foundational theology.[4] This area was the focus of his teaching career, but his writing and many of his lectures dealt with ecclesiology, which will be a focus of this chapter.

A good place to begin is to look at his methodology. Throughout his academic career, Dulles basically employed two kinds of methodologies, namely, typology and the use of models. Typology is a means of classification. For example, topics may be arranged according to specific themes, to authors holding similar viewpoints, or to historical periods, to cite but a few. From the beginning of his academic career, Dulles displayed a fondness for this way of organizing his material. His usual procedure was to group various theologians together according to prechosen similarities, present their insights in a systematic fashion, and then to compare and contrast each type with the others. From the viewpoint of typological methodology, Dulles appeared to be more of a commentator on the positions of other theologians rather than an innovator in his own right. Commenting on this method, Dulles gave us an insight into his own personality: "Characteristically reflective by temperament, typologists seek to avoid the fray and reconcile the warring parties. Conscious of the partial perspectives of others, they wish to keep their options open."[5]

Dulles popularized the use of models in theology, a methodology originally used in the fields of the physical and social sciences.[6] In his theological system, a model may be described as "a relatively simple, artificially constructed case which is found to be useful and illuminating for dealing with realities that are more complex and differentiated."[7] Models provide the opportunity of describing those things that do not readily admit of precise definitions, of comparing diverse opinions, and of critically assessing data.

To understand Dulles's use of models in his works, it is necessary to begin with his appreciation of the centrality of mystery in theology. Mystery is at the core of all Dulles's theological undertakings, and the models approach was his way of protecting and respecting this element of mystery. Because mystery cannot be captured once and for all, the experience of it must be interpreted using analogies. The analogies chosen to express a specific dimension of mystery lead to their articulation in images. Images provide an important service to the concept of mystery, because not all truth can be explored in a completely literal fashion.

Images then lead to the creation of models, and Dulles saw an integral connection between image and model: "When an image is employed reflectively and critically to deepen one's theoretical understanding of a reality it becomes what is today called a 'model.'"[8]

Dulles classified models in two ways: (1) explanatory, which synthesize what is already known, and (2) exploratory, which have the capacity to lead to new theological insights.[9] His use of models may then be summarized in the following ways. The experience of mystery is interpreted through analogies that are expressed in images. These images are then constructed into models. Or, coming from another direction, experience may be classified by means of the selection of types, with ideal types becoming models.[10] While this approach is the basis of his two books that feature the word *model* in their titles (*Models of the Church* and *Models of Revelation*), it also forms the basis of many of the articles Dulles published.

A major asset in using models in theology is to maintain a healthy pluralism, which is a hallmark of his theological method. Dulles believed that the various models used to illustrate a theological concept must be kept in dialectical tension with one another, and that each should be used to critique and complement the others. To choose only one as paradigmatic would lead to distortion.[11]

For many people, the name Avery Dulles has become almost synonymous with the term "models of the Church," as this is the title of the book in which he presented the rich insights of *Lumen Gentium* and the other ecclesiological pronouncements of Vatican II. The impact of this book in our country was nothing short of phenomenal. Avery Dulles and his models approach became, if not a household name, at least popular among the clergy, religious educators, and Catholic intelligentsia. Those who did not read *Models of the Church* themselves were introduced to its concepts through their pastors and parish personnel.

What was the reason for the immense popularity of this small book? Much of the credit for its widespread acceptance must be attributed to the way in which it was written. First, Dulles had a tremendous sense of history, enabling him to situate the only experience of Church most of his readers would have had within the larger framework of the experience of Christianity's almost two thousand years of existence. Second, he was able to find good and bad points in each of his models, thus easing the transition to the broader vision of the Council's presentation of the Church. Last, but by no means least, the scholarly investigations and conclusions were presented in a very sensitive manner. One must remember the tenor of the times of the early 1970s. It was a period of confusion and disillusionment, as previous structures, both in Church and in society, were being questioned. This process of reevaluation led to very painful polarizations, as many people became enmeshed in their own viewpoints and refused to investigate any other options. Dulles's adamant opposition of any type of polarization in the Church is at the basis of the sensitivity one finds in his style.

As previously stated, an affirmation of mystery lies at the very heart of all Dulles's work in theology. Therefore, it comes as no surprise that his ecclesiology was based on this same premise. He presented the Church as a multifaceted reality, one that cannot be limited to any specific frame of reference. Because the essence of the Church is rooted in mystery, it will always be greater than any attempt to describe it. For this reason, Dulles pursued his preferred path of working simultaneously with several complementary images and models.

Dulles pleaded for an integration of the Church as institution, communion, sacrament, herald, and servant, for it is only by looking at these five models in their mutuality and totality, that the divine/human aspect of the Church can clearly be seen. However, five must not be viewed as some sort of magical number, for Dulles observed, "The number of models may be varied almost at will. In some presentations I have invoked as many as seven or eight. For simplicity's sake, I find it better to work with as few as possible."[12] Although a more detailed explanation of the models has been outlined elsewhere in this book, it would be useful to present here a brief description of each of the models.

The institution model highlights the Church as a visible society, hierarchically structured, instituted by Jesus Christ, which communicates salvation by authoritative doctrine, ministry of sacraments, and pastoral care. This was the predominant way the Church was experienced by most Catholics before Vatican II. The second model, community, emphasizes the Church as the people of God (or Mystical Body) bound together by fellowship in the Spirit. The third of Dulles's models presents the sacramental image, in which the Church is seen as the visible sign and embodiment of Christ's redemptive presence and work. The herald model portrays the Church as the missionary society sent to evangelize the world. And the last of Dulles's five models sees the Church as servant, an agent for social change whose task is to collaborate with God in the transformation of the world into God's kingdom.

Although a cursory sketch of the five models of the Church, it nonetheless gives you a flavor for the richness contained in an encompassing vision of the Church. While none of the models should be considered the one and only way to approach the mystery of the Church, Dulles had hinted in *Models of the Church* that, of the five considered, the sacramental model might be the best vehicle for the integration of the others.[13] In his next book, *The Resilient Church* (1977), his thinking evolved to the point where he clearly and unequivocally expressed his preference for viewing the Church as sacrament. Quoting Vatican II's description of the Church as "the universal sacrament of salvation" (*LG* 48), he boldly asserts, "after some years of work in ecclesiology, I am inclined to think that there is no better definition."[14] In *A Church to Believe In*, published in 1982, Dulles admits that "in contemporary ecclesiology the concept of sacrament is prominent."[15] However, he realized the limitations of that model: "This may not be the kind of image that can easily be popularized in our time."[16]

In this book, therefore, Dulles proposed a new model, namely, the Church as a community of disciples.[17] He presented the Church as a community that gathers in the presence of Jesus and imitates the first disciples. Furthermore, the Church is the place that authentic discipleship—the response to the call of God—remains possible. This image has a strong biblical foundation, for while theologians are grappling with the question of whether or not Jesus did in fact establish the Church, he did assemble a group of disciples around himself. "'Community of disciples' is precisely what Jesus undoubtedly did found, and once we recognize this fact we can apply to our life in the Church many of the Gospel passages dealing with discipleship."[18] However valid and fruitful this contemporary application to ecclesiology may be, Dulles himself cautioned against a canonization of it: "I would not go so far as to assert that the discipleship model can be used to take the place of all the others. As a mystery, the Church is irreducible to any single concept or image."[19]

Vatican II called for a renewed vision of the Church that would include a plurality of images, none of which would be taken as exhaustive. By condensing the most predominant of these images into his five models, Dulles popularized this aspect of Vatican II's ecclesiology, and literally made it accessible to "the person in the pew." However, in his reflections on the postconciliar Church, Dulles realized that this vision has not yet been attained. In *A Church to Believe In*, Dulles notes that the Church was still commonly experienced in terms of its institutional components alone,[20] and the situation had not drastically changed since then, although a quarter of a century had passed since he wrote that book.

Why haven't the beautiful images of the Church, as portrayed in *Lumen Gentium*, taken root in the self-understanding of the faithful? In evaluating the three central images—Body of Christ, people of God, and sacrament—Dulles found an answer in the fact that none of these resonate with lived experience.[21] For this reason, he proposed the discipleship model, which, in his opinion, is true to both the teachings of Vatican II and to contemporary life. However, the potential promise Dulles saw in the discipleship model has not been realized either. He himself did not pursued it, except in occasional references. Perhaps, despite its inherent merits, the discipleship model also does not reflect the lived situation of most Roman Catholics today.

The teachings of Vatican II have served as the focal point not only of Dulles's ecclesiology, but of his entire theological system. His book *The Reshaping of Catholicism* (1988) is a collection of essays that deal specifically with the Church in light of Vatican II.[22] In that same year, he acknowledged in an interview with Peter Steinfels in the *New York Times* that "what I've been doing these last 20, 25 years really centers around interpreting Vatican II."[23] As time progressed, it seems that he emphasized the conciliar documents more intensely in an attempt to challenge the Church to a greater fidelity to its mission.

There was a tendency to interpret the documents of Vatican II as calling for more secularist and political types of theology. This was especially true in the years immediately following the Council. *Gaudium et Spes* called for "reading the signs of the times." Dulles agreed with this injunction, but he also cautioned against becoming so overly identified with its surroundings that the Church loses its identity. In very simple words, he issued the challenge "Let the Church become the Church!"[24] This sentence aptly describes his motivation through the years. While he was fully convinced of the Church's need for adaptation and renewal, he did not endorse any changes that would detract from its true mission as a sacrament of Christ's presence in the world. Not everything that would call itself Christian is worthy of the designation. Choices must be made to ensure the Church's fidelity to its vocation.

He said, "We may say that the Council repeatedly and emphatically taught that the procurement of salvation is the most important task of the church."[25] The very reason for the Church's presence in the world is its existence as the "universal sacrament of salvation" (*LG* 1; *GS* 45; *AG* 1). According to Vatican II, the sanctification of humankind is especially present in the Church's liturgy (*SC* 7), forming the basis of the Church's mission to evangelize (*LG* 17; *AG* 7) and to hasten the reunification of the one true Church (*UR* 4).

If salvation is viewed as the most important task of the Church, it follows that service within the Church must be directed to this end. Dulles did not believe that Vatican II intended that such service be oriented primarily to the betterment of the social order. In fact, his opinions were quite the contrary. He clearly distinguished between what is "proper" to the Church's mission and the repercussions that flow from this mission, defining the former as "that which is specific to the church and would remain undone unless the church existed."[26] In this category, he placed preaching faith in Christ and administering the sacraments. Naturally, the living of an authentic faith relationship with Christ and the deepening of this graced relationship with him sacramentally will lead his followers to strive for justice for all persons. Yet that is a result of the Church's salvific activity, not its cause. Dulles made a subtle distinction in claiming that, while the erection of a just society is not proper to the Church, contributing to this society is.[27]

A VOICE OF MODERATION

While other theologians may have been constructing highly innovative systems, especially in the years immediately following Vatican II, Dulles was quietly and unassumingly pursuing his own path as the "voice of moderation." Throughout all his writings, Dulles tried to maintain a mediating position between conservative and liberal viewpoints. He attempted to present a balanced view of the issues at hand, describing the assets and liabilities of each side. He was grieved at the polarization that has occurred since Vatican II and tried to escape being labeled as either a conservative or a liberal. This was Dulles's chosen course, and one that he long cherished. In the interview with Peter Steinfels previously quoted, Dulles reiterated his personal goal when he stated, "I would like to be a kind of bridge person."[28] His writings have indeed served as a bridge over the troubled waters of the post–Vatican II Church.

Dulles was aware that his interpretation of the teachings of Vatican II can be viewed as ecclesiocentric, yet he maintained his position. His years of research and reflection on the conciliar documents led him to conclude that "the Council does not regard the world as the center and the church as peripheral, but rather the reverse."[29]

Dulles achieved an international reputation for his lucid and prudent insights in ecclesiology. But it would be a mistake to limit his ecclesiology to the Roman Catholic Church. Dulles was involved in the ecumenical movement even before this participation was encouraged by Vatican II. During his formation period as a Jesuit, he was deeply influenced by Gustave Weigel, SJ, who was a leading figure in the preconciliar ecumenical movement in America. Weigel conveyed to Dulles his own passion for the unity of the Church, a passion that grasped Dulles for over six decades. This enthusiasm might seem to have an autobiographical referent, but this is not the case. Dulles himself once suggested to Weigel that ecumenism would be a good area for him to explore, based on his own background as a convert. Weigel insisted that this fact alone would not suffice; rather, anyone wishing to pursue ecumenical theology would need to be personally convinced of its inherent worth.

In the late 1950s, Dulles was sent to Germany and then to Rome to study the thinking of Protestant theologians. In 1960, he completed his doctoral dissertation, "Protestant Church and the Prophetic Office." Thus, Dulles had a solid preparation for the teachings of Vatican II on ecumenism. His participation in ecumenical affairs is attested to by the fact that he was a member of the Archdiocese of Baltimore's Commission on Christian Unity (1962–70), a consultor to the Papal Secretariat for Dialogue with Non-Believers (1966–73), and a member of the United States Lutheran-Roman Catholic Dialogue, the Anglican-Roman Catholic Consultation in the United States, and a member of Evangelicals and Catholics Together. He contributed to the Lutheran-Roman Catholic Joint Statements on the "Papacy" (1974), "Teaching Authority and Infallibility in the Church" (1978), "Justification" (1983), and "The One Mediator, the Saints and Mary" (1990); the Anglican-Roman Catholic statement on "Doctrinal Agreement and Christian Unity" (1972); and the World Council of Churches' study paper, "Baptism, Eucharist and Ministry" (1982).

In addition to interacting with other theologians while serving on the previously named commissions, Dulles's dialogue with others primarily took place in his writings. His style was to present the teachings of his colleagues, Catholic and non-Catholic, in the theological community, both past and present, and then to explain and evaluate their positions. This ability to synthesize, explore, and critique many divergent opinions forms a large part of Dulles's contribution to the cause of the unity of the Church.

The texts of Vatican II that had the most profound influence on Dulles's thinking are *Lumen Gentium* 8 and *Unitatis Redintegratio* 11. These important conciliar pronouncements have been quoted often through the years, but here we stress a sentence in each passage that is less well known, but which has nonetheless had a profound influence on Dulles's theology.

When speaking of the Church of Christ, *Lumen Gentium* states,

This Church constituted and organized in the world as a society, subsists in the Catholic Church, which is governed by the successor of Peter and by the Bishops in union with him, although many elements of sanctification and of truth can be found outside of her visible structure. These elements, as gifts

properly belonging to the Church of Christ, are forces impelling toward Catholic unity. (no. 8)

The meaning of "subsists" in this famous passage continues to be
discussed; however, it is the last sentence of this paragraph that specifically influenced Dulles's theology. How would he identify these elements
that are gifts of the Church of Christ? His answer would point to the
heritage of the other churches. He did not ask any church to renounce
its history, its distinctiveness, nor the means it offers to lead its members
to God. Rather, he advocated incorporating individual emphases with
those of the other churches to provide more balance. This type of
endeavor brings us back again to one of Dulles's favorite themes—that of
catholicity. His "both/and" attitude allowed for great flexibility in
thought and practice, and certainly held more ecumenical potential than
the more rigid "either/or."

But this does not mean that Dulles's ecumenical thrust was based
on a syncretic indifference, an "anything goes" mentality. He believed
that the differences among the churches cannot be overcome by denying
them, ignoring them, or minimizing them. Only a frank and honest
appraisal of the situation holds the possibility for true ecumenism. This is
the theme of the other conciliar passage, which, in my opinion, is at the
core of Dulles's ecumenical theology. *Unitatis Redintegratio* contains the
oft-quoted statement about the "hierarchy" of truths, which has been
important in Dulles's theology. However, earlier in this same document,
we find the following sentence: "Nothing is so foreign to the spirit of
ecumenism as a false conciliatory approach which harms the purity of
Catholic doctrine and obscures its assured genuine meaning" (no. 11).

To this end, Dulles did not sanction premature reunion or pretend
that more unity exists than presently does. He called for patient endeavor
in the ecumenical movement, knowing full well that total reunion will
require much time and effort. In the meantime, however, he gave suggestions that are realistic embodiments of a true conciliatory approach.

Total communion is the goal toward which the churches are tend-
ing, but Dulles did not believe that it will be achieved in an immediate
fashion; rather, he anticipated reunion occurring in three stages. The first
of these concerns the preparation and publication of a joint statement,

indicating the churches' belief in Scripture and in the creeds of the early ecumenical councils. This would be followed by an acceptance of each other's doctrinal positions as not contrary to the gospel, with an accompanying lifting of anathemas where necessary. The last step would be the acceptance of the binding doctrinal declarations of the other churches, with whatever explanatory statements are needed.[30]

Once again, we see evidences of the catholicity approach. For Dulles, ecumenism was both an acceptance of the here-and-now reality of imperfect communion, and an impetus toward perfecting that communion. Therefore, he did not believe that intercommunion is an appropriate expression at this time, given the divided state of the churches. He proposed several liturgical alternatives that are intended to sharpen our awareness of the present situation, for example, prayerful abstention from the Eucharist celebrated in another church and ritualizing the pain of disunity.[31] These suggestions, viewed in light of Dulles's teachings on symbol and mystery, are powerful reminders that there is much yet to be done before the Church is truly one.

Dulles used the phrase "creative fidelity"[32] to describe the connection between continuity and change in the Church. My research and analysis of various developments in his ecclesiological and ecumenical theologies indicate that this is an apt description of his writings. If he placed more weight on one side, it was concerning continuity in the tradition. As already stated, his creativity is to be found more in how he presented the tradition and reformulated it for the contemporary scene than in devising new theories.

Avery Dulles is the most influential of all contemporary American theologians. Through his painstaking research, his reflection and dialogue, and his clear and concise writings, he has opened our minds and our hearts to the beauty and richness of many aspects of our faith heritage. The Church, in general, and the Church in America, in particular, would be greatly impoverished without his contributions.

NOTES

INTRODUCTION

1. Avery Dulles, *Models of Revelation* (Maryknoll, NY: Orbis, 1992).

2. Avery Dulles, *Models of the Church*, exp. ed. (Garden City, NY: Image Books, 1987).

3. See Robert Bellarmine, *De Controversilis*, tom. 2, lib. 3, cap. 2 (Naples: Giuliano, 1857), 2:75. Cited in *Models of the Church*.

4. Avery Dulles, *Models of the Church* (New York: Doubleday and Company, 1974), 31.

5. Dulles, *Models of the Church*, 45.

6. Dulles, *Models of the Church*, 51.

7. Henri de Lubac, *Catholicism* (London: Burns, Oates and Washbourne, 1950), 29.

8. See Paul McPartlan, *The Eucharist Makes the Church: Henri de Lubac and John Zizioulas in Dialogue* (London: T&T Clark, 1993).

9. Dulles, *Models of the Church* (1974), 71.

10. Richard McBrien, *Church: The Continuing Quest* (New York: Newman, 1970), 11.

11. Karl Barth, *Church Dogmatics*, vol. 1, pt. 1 (Edinburgh: T&T Clark, 1936), 298–300.

12. Dulles, *Models of the Church* (1974), 85–86. The length of this quote is necessary due to the complexity of this model and its methodology.

13. Dulles, *Models of the Church* (1974), 13–30.

14. Guido Pozzo, "Method: Systematic Theology," in *Dictionary of Fundamental Theology*, ed. René Latourelle and Rino Fisichella (New York: Crossroad Publishing Company, 1994), 670.

15. See I. T. Ramsey, *Religious Language* (New York: Macmillan Paperbacks, 1963); I. T. Ramsey, *Models and Mystery* (New York: Oxford University Press, 1964); Max Black, *Models and Metaphors* (Ithaca: Cornell University Press, 1962).

On the theology of symbol, see F. W. Dillistone, ed., *Myth and Symbol* (London: SCM, 1970), and Karl Rahner, "The Theology of Symbol," in *Theological Investigations*, vol. 4, trans. Cornelius Ernst (Baltimore: Helicon, 1966), 221–52. Also, Avery Dulles, "Symbol in Revelation," in *New Catholic Encyclopedia*, vol. 13 (Washington, DC: The Catholic University of America, 1967): 861–63. On the sociology of symbol, see Kenneth E. Boulding, *The Image* (Ann Arbor: University of Michigan Press, 1956); Robert N. Bellah, "Transcendence in Contemporary Piety," in *Beyond Belief* (New York: Harper and Row, 1970), 196–208; P. Minear, *Images of the Church in the New Testament* (Philadelphia: Westminster Press, 1960), 24; and E. Cousins, "Models and the Future of Theology," *Continuum* 7 (1969): 78–91.

16. See Stephan Meier-Oeser, "Medieval Semiotics," in *The Stanford Encyclopedia of Philosophy* (Winter 2003 edition), ed. Edward N. Zalta, accessed May 21, 2018, https://plato.stanford.edu/entries/semiotics-medieval/.

17. Dulles, *Models of the Church* (1974), 21.

18. *Lumen Gentium*, no. 1. See also Avery Dulles, "Introduction and Commentary on The Church," in *The Documents of Vatican II*, ed. Walter M. Abbott (New York: Herder and Herder, 1966), 14. In his commentary in the footnotes of the Abbot edition, Dulles writes that the term *mystery* indicates that the Church, as a divine reality inserted into history, cannot be fully captured by human thought or language. As Paul VI said in his opening allocution at the second session (September 29, 1963), "The Church is a mystery. It is a reality imbued with the hidden presence of God. It lies, therefore, within the very nature of the Church to be always open to new and greater exploration."

19. *Lumen Gentium*, beginning in paragraph six, and in the following four paragraphs, develops the various biblical metaphors into images of the Church. Dulles notes that "these images, taken from different spheres of human life (pastoral life, agriculture, building and matrimony), magnificently supplement one another and indicate in different ways Christ's tender love for, and intimate union with, the Church."

20. Pozzo, "Method: Systematic Theology," 670.

21. Pozzo, "Method: Systematic Theology," 670.

22. Ewert Cousins, "Models and the Future of Theology," *Continuum* 7 (1969): 78–91.

23. To be distinguished here is the term "secular theological method" from what Dulles has called the "secular dialogic method." The former refers to what is more commonly called liberal theology as opposed to the latter that can be a way of doing Catholic theology, after the example of *Gaudium et Spes*. For

a thorough treatment of liberal theology, which sees its project as charting a middle course between orthodoxy on one hand and rationalistic deism/atheism on the other, see Gary J. Dorrien's magisterial work *The Making of American Liberal Theology*: vol. 1, *Imagining Progressive Religion 1805–1900*, vol. 2, *Idealism, Realism and Modernity, 1900–1950*, and vol. 3, *Crisis, Irony and Post-Modernity, 1950–2005* (Louisville, KY: Westminster/John Knox, 2001–06).

24. Cousins, "Models and the Future of Theology," 81.

25. Cousins, "Models and the Future of Theology," 82.

26. Pozzo, "Method: Systematic Theology," 670.

27. I am referring to what has come to be called the experiential expressive school, which holds, following Mircea Eliade and Carl Gustav Jung, that religion is at its base an experience of the single, numinous reality of the divine. According to this school, everything is grounded in a single, mystical experience, out from which emerges the world religions, different in the cultural expression of the one experience, but finally united *in radice.*

28. Cousins, "Models and the Future of Theology," 83–84. Cousins, it should be noted, moderates the experiential expressive approach by a call for a return to the early Christian experience as expressed in the Scripture as a corrective to the problem of either letting expressive models get too elaborate or by focusing on the wrong level of experience. Still, I would argue that a theory of religion that posits a mystical ground of unity beneath all religions sets up difficulties for theology in a revealed religion.

29. See Joas Adiprasetya, "George A. Lindbeck and Postliberal Theology," in *Boston Collaborative Encyclopedia of Modern Western Theology*, 2005, accessed March 10, 2008, http://people.bu.edu/wwildman/WeirdWildWeb/courses/ mwt/dictionary/mwt_themes_862_lindbeck.htm. For Barth, as is well known, all religion is human invention as opposed to the revealed faith of Christianity. Religion, for Barth, has no theological status. As Paul Cassel notes, "The metaphor of the tangent shows that Barth specifically rejected both human spiritual experience and self-consciousness as a guide to God and regarded both Christian and non-Christian religion as failed attempts to abide at the point of tangency."

30. Dulles, *Models of the Church* (1974), 23.

31. See Thomas A. Baima, *The Concordat of Agreement between the Episcopal Church and the Evangelical Lutheran Church in America: Lessons on the Way toward Full Communion* (Lampeter, Wales: Edwin Mellen Press, 2003).

32. Thomas A. Baima, "The Use of Heuristic Theory in the Study of the Evangelical Lutheran Church in America" (paper presented at the Midwest American Academy of Religion, Chicago, Illinois, April 6, 2002).

33. J. Edward Russo and Paul J. H. Schoemaker, *Decision Traps: The Ten Barriers to Brilliant Decision-Making and How to Overcome Them* (New York: Simon and Schuster, 1989), 227. See also, Daniel Kahneman and Amos Tversky, "Judgment under Uncertainty: Heuristics and Biases," *Science* 185 (1974): 1124–31; "Framing of Decisions and the Psychology of Choice," *Science* 211 (1981): 453–58; "The Psychology of Preferences," *Scientific American* (January 1982): 160–73; Robyn M. Daves, *Rational Choice in an Uncertain World* (New York: Harcourt, Brace Jovanovich, 1988); Robin Hogarth, *Judgment and Choice*, 2nd ed. (New York: John Wiley and Sons, 1987); Daniel Kahneman, Paul Slovic, and Amos Tversky, *Judgment under Uncertainty and Biases* (Cambridge: Cambridge University Press, 1986); Hal R. Arkes and Kenneth R. Hammond, eds., *Judgment and Decision-Making: An Interdisciplinary Reader* (Cambridge: Cambridge University Press, 1986); David Bell, Howard Raiffa, and Amos Tversky, *Decision-Making: Description, Normative and Prescriptive Interactions* (Cambridge: Cambridge University Press, 1988).

34. John S. Hammond, Ralph L. Keeney, and Howard Raiffa, "The Hidden Traps in Decision Making," *Harvard Business Review* 76, no. 5 (September–October 1998): 47.

35. Hammond, Keeney, and Raiffa, "The Hidden Traps in Decision Making," 48.

36. Hans Küng, *My Struggle for Freedom: Memoirs* (Grand Rapids, MI: William B. Eerdmans Publishing Company, 2002), 370.

37. Hammond, Keeney, and Raiffa, "The Hidden Traps in Decision Making," 48.

38. Hammond, Keeney, and Raiffa, "The Hidden Traps in Decision Making," 50.

39. The "Profession of Faith" of Msgr. Marcel Lefebvre was made public in Rome on November 21, 1974.

40. Hammond, Keeney, and Raiffa, "The Hidden Traps in Decision Making," 50.

41. Hammond, Keeney, and Raiffa, "The Hidden Traps in Decision Making," 52.

42. Hammond, Keeney, and Raiffa, "The Hidden Traps in Decision Making," 54. See also Amos Tversky and Daniel Kahneman, "The Framing of Decisions and the Psychology of Choice," *Science* 211 (January 1981): 453–57;

DeWitt C. Dearborn and Herbert A. Simon, "Selective Perception: A Note on the Departmental Identification of Executives," *Sociometry* 21 (1958): 140–44; Peter Drucker, *Management: Tasks, Responsibilities, Practices* (New York: Harper and Row, 1974); Max H. Bazerman, "The Relevance of Kahneman and Tversky's Concept of Framing to Organizational Behavior," *Journal of Management* 10, no. 3 (Fall/Winter 1984): 333–43. Howard Raiffa, *The Art and Science of Negotiation* (Cambridge, MA: Harvard University Press, 1982).

43. Hammond, Keeney, and Raiffa, "The Hidden Traps in Decision Making," 53–54.

44. Dulles, *Models of the Church* (1974), 29.

45. Avery Dulles, *A Church to Believe In: Discipleship and the Dynamics of Freedom* (New York: Crossroad, 1982).

46. See Thomas A. Baima, "Polarization in the Church," *Seminary Journal* 8, no. 1 (2002).

47. William H. Willimon, *What's Right with the Church* (San Francisco: Harper and Row, 1985), 36.

48. Avery Dulles, *Models of the Church*, exp. ed., 208–9.

49. Avery Dulles, *Models of the Church*, 209–10.

50. Avery Dulles, *Models of the Church*, 218.

51. Avery Dulles, *Models of the Church*, 222.

52. For more on the issue of contemporary polarization, see Thomas A. Baima, "Polarization in the Church," *Seminary Journal* 8, no. 1 (Spring 2002).

53. *Unitatis Redintegratio* 4 described this method as follows: "These are: first, every effort to avoid expressions, judgments and actions which do not represent the condition of our separated brethren with truth and fairness and so make mutual relations with them more difficult; then, 'dialogue' between competent experts from different Churches and Communities. At these meetings, which are organized in a religious spirit, each explains the teaching of his Communion in greater depth and brings out clearly its distinctive features. In such dialogue, everyone gains a truer knowledge and more just appreciation of the teaching and religious life of both Communions." See http://www.vatican.va/archive/hist_councils/ii_vatican_council/documents/vat-ii_decree_19641121_unitatis-redintegratio_en.html (accessed March 18, 2008).

54. John Paul II, speaking to Mar Dinkha in 1994, noted that the *Common Christological Declaration* was possible because "at the time of your previous visit, you shared with me your ardent wish that a declaration of the Pope of Rome and of the Catholicos-Patriarch of the Assyrian Church of the East would one day be able to express our two Churches' common faith in Jesus Christ, the Incarnate

Son of God, born of the Virgin Mary. Historians and theologians immediately set about examining very carefully the Christological consequences of the Council of Ephesus. In an atmosphere of fraternity and mutual confidence, a fruitful dialogue has enabled us to overcome the ambiguities and misunderstandings of the past. Today, we have arrived at the *Common Christological Declaration* which we are about to sign together. This constitutes an important witness which will not fail to cause rejoicing among the faithful of our two Churches." See http://www .vatican.va/holy_father/john_paul_ii/speeches/1994/november/documents/hf _jp-ii_spe_19941111_chiesa-assira_en.html (accessed March 17, 2008).

55. See James M. Kushiner et al., "Plausible Ecumenism: An Ecumenical Roundtable Discussion," *Touchstone* 13, no. 1 (January/February 2000). See also Richard John Neuhaus, "That They May Be One: Prospects for Unity in the Twenty-First Century," *Touchstone* (July/August 2003).

56. Center for Catholic and Evangelical Theology, *In One Body through the Cross: The Princeton Proposal for Christian Unity; A Call to the Churches from an Ecumenical Study Group* (Grand Rapids, MI: Eerdmans, 2003).

57. Kushiner et al., "Plausible Ecumenism," 21.

58. *Oxford English Dictionary*. It is interesting that, if you trace the etymology of the word, you also find in the noun forms the notion of a boundary, or limit, and the notion of right (correct).

59. *First Things* (May 1994).

60. *First Things* (January 1998).

61. *Your Word is Truth* (Grand Rapids, MI: Eerdmans, 2002). See also *First Things* (August/September 2002).

62. *First Things* (March 2003).

63. *First Things* (March 2005).

64. *Pro Oriente Syriac Dialogue Series*, vols. 1–6 (Vienna: Foundation Pro Oriente, 1994–2004).

65. See Tom J. Nettles, Richard L. Pratt, and Robert Kolb, *Understanding Four Views on Baptism* (Grand Rapids, MI: Zondervan, 2007). See also, Russell D. Moore, I. John Hesselink, David Scaer, and Thomas A. Baima, *Understanding Four Views on the Lord's Supper* (Grand Rapids, MI: Zondervan, 2007).

66. *Unitatis Redintegratio*, no. 9.

1. THEOLOGIAN OF THE CHURCH

1. Avery Dulles, *Princeps Concordiae: Pico della Mirandola and the Scholastic Tradition* (Cambridge, MA: Harvard University Press, 1941).

2. The survey of Pico's works, Dulles, *Princeps Concordiae*, 11–24, is an example of such thoroughness.

3. Dulles, *Princeps Concordiae*, 25–45. That is so even if we later discover that Pico's doctrine of the world-soul—and consequently his espousal of "natural magic" (hence the role of the Cabbala)—derives from the Hermetic literature: Dulles, *Princeps Concordiae*, 89. (For Pico, "natural causes were themselves intelligent, insofar as they participated in the universal soul.")

4. Dulles, *Princeps Concordiae*, 60. By the end of his chapter on Pico's psychology and epistemology, however, Dulles seems to lose patience momentarily with Pico's eclecticism. Pico's account of the intellect is "one of his many rather exasperating attempts to combine irreconcilable elements in his philosophy." Yet four sentences later, Pico's epistemology is deemed a "quest for a *pax philosophica* founded upon the most honoured realistic traditions of Greek, Arabic, and Latin thought," 143.

5. Dulles, *Princeps Concordiae*, 3.

6. Dulles, *Princeps Concordiae*, 77.

7. Avery Dulles, *The Catholicity of the Church* (Oxford: Clarendon Press, 1985).

8. Avery Dulles, *The Assurance of Things Hoped For: A Theology of Christian Faith* (New York: Oxford University Press, 1994).

9. Avery Dulles, J. M. Demske, and R. J. O'Connell, *Introductory Metaphysics* (New York: Sheed & Ward, 1955). A fruit of the years as "Instructor of Philosophy" at Fordham, which followed his military service in the Second World War and entry into the Society of Jesus.

10. Dulles, *Princeps Concordiae*, 154.

11. Dulles, *Princeps Concordiae*, 156.

12. Avery Dulles, *A History of Apologetics* (New York: Corpus Instrumentorum, 1971; 2nd ed., San Francisco: Ignatius Press, 2005); Avery Dulles, *Apologetics and the Biblical Christ* (London: Burns & Oates, 1964).

13. Avery Dulles, *Newman* (London: Continuum, 2002), 34–63.

14. Dulles, *Princeps Concordiae*, 154. Dulles refers the reader here to the English translation of the second edition of Gilson's study *The Philosophy of S. Thomas Aquinas* (London: B. Herder Book Company, 1937), and to Gilson's *Reason and Revelation in the Middle Ages* (New York: C. Scribner's Sons, 1938).

15. Avery Dulles, *The Craft of Theology: From Symbol to System* (Dublin: Gill and Macmillan, 1992); Avery Dulles, *Revelation Theology: A History* (London: Burns & Oates, 1970); Avery Dulles, *Models of Revelation* (Garden City, NY: Doubleday, 1983).

16. Avery Dulles, *The Resilient Church:The Necessity and Limits of Adaptation* (Dublin: Gill and Macmillan, 1977); Avery Dulles, *The Reshaping of Catholicism: Current Challenges in the Theology of Church* (San Francisco: Harper & Row, 1988).

17. Avery Dulles, *Models of the Church*, 2nd ed. (Dublin: Gill and Macmillan, 1988). See also Avery Dulles, *A Testimonial to Grace and Reflections on a Theological Journey*, 50th anniv. ed. (Kansas City, MO: Sheed & Ward, 1996), 118. In the former, Dulles explained how a "general theory of sacramentality" drawn from philosophical and theological anthropology can yield a theology of the Church once "philosophical considerations are transposed to the supernatural plane" (65). Even the "heavenly Church" will exist as a "sum total of signs" (115). Dulles's concern with cosmic catholicity emerges when he avers that, in the new heavens and new earth of biblical eschatology, "the glorious, triumphant Church will be indivisibly united with the renewed cosmos" (121).

18. Dulles, *Revelation Theology: A History*, 135.

19. Dulles, *Revelation Theology*, 9.

20. Dulles, *Revelation Theology*.

21. Dulles, *Revelation Theology*, 11.

22. Etienne Gilson, *Index scolastico-cartésien* (Paris: J.Vrin, 1918).

23. See Ross A. Shecterle, *The Theology of Revelation of Avery Dulles 1980–1994* (Lewiston, NY: Edwin Mellen Press, 1996), 203: "It could be argued that Dulles occasionally slips into a 'cognitive-propositional' approach, one which perceives symbols as subordinate to propositional speech." In his study of revelation via models, Dulles had drawn attention to the "importance of doctrine in clarifying the ambiguities in symbolic communication, whether verbal or non-verbal" (*Models of Revelation*, 222).

24. Dulles, *Revelation Theology*, 74.

25. For all Dulles's awareness of contemporary theological movements, the greater part of his discussion of the nature, object, grounding, and properties of faith in that study derive from Scholastic discussion and the magisterial tradition, except possibly for his account of faith's "obscurity," where the Fathers and medieval monastic theologians are brought briefly into play. See *The Assurance of Things Hoped For*, 235.

26. John Henry Newman, *University Sermons: Fifteen Sermons Preached before the University of Oxford, 1826–1843*, 3rd ed. (London: Society for Promoting Christian Knowledge, 1970), 239.

27. H. Tristram, "Cardinal Newman's *Theses de Fide* and His Proposed Introduction to the French Translation of the University Sermons," *Gregorianum* 18 (1937): 219–60.

28. Dulles, *Revelation Theology*, 72.

29. Pierre Rousselot, *The Eyes of Faith and Answer to Two Attacks*, trans. John M. McDermott and Avery Dulles (New York: Fordham University Press, 1991), 21–81.

30. Rousselot, *The Eyes of Faith and Answer to Two Attacks*, 28.

31. Dulles, *Apologetics and the Biblical Christ*, 62.

32. Avery Dulles, *A Testimonial to Grace* (New York: Sheed & Ward, 1946).

33. Dulles, *Apologetics and the Biblical Christ*, 95, referring to Jean Levie, *Sous les Yeux de l'incroyant*, 2nd ed. (Brussels: Desclee de Brouwer, 1946). In *A History of Apologetics*, Dulles speaks of the very person of Christ as "the primary sign of credibility, to judge from the Gospels," though he acknowledges the role of the miracles as "secondary signs, not wholly separable from the person and work of Jesus" (2).

34. We should note, though, how subsequently Dulles enters a caveat in Rousselot's regard. While Rousselot's theory has "many merits," attention must be paid to the Dominican critics, ranging from Reginald Garrigou-Lagrange to Yves Congar, who regretted his refusal to make a sharper distinction between faith and its rational grounds in what the eyes of faith see (thus, Dulles, *The Assurance of Things Hoped For*, 111). Dulles became especially wary of what he termed the "radicalization of the trend inaugurated by Blondel and Rousselot" in Karl Rahner's theology of faith, for which the light of faith is itself "a kind of subjective or transcendental revelation…permitting an act of faith even when unaccompanied by the explicit transmission of any specific revealed truths" (153).

35. Dulles, *Revelation Theology*, 77.

36. At a time when some Catholic writers sought to rehabilitate the Modernists, notably Tyrrell, Dulles calls Catholic Modernism quite frankly "in substance, a Catholic echo of [the] Protestant theology of the late nineteenth century," notably in the latter's influencing by Neo-Kantian agnosticism, Neo-Hegelian evolutionary pantheism, and pragmatist vitalism. The cost Modernists would have been willing to pay was, in one of Dulles's understated formulae, "a certain discontinuity with the Church's own past teaching and institutional forms" (*Revelation Theology*, 83).

37. Dulles, *Revelation Theology*, 87.

38. "While asserting the capacity of human reason to establish the preambles of faith, including the existence of God, the pope recognized the indispensability of moral dispositions and the important role of knowledge 'by connaturality.' While defending the validity of Scholastic theology, he praised

the biblical movement, and noted that theology grows barren when it does not constantly nourish itself from the original sources" (*Revelation Theology*, 153).

39. Cited in Dulles, *Revelation Theology*, 22.

40. Dulles, *Revelation Theology*, 26.

41. Dulles, *Revelation Theology*, 28, with reference to 1 John 3:2.

42. Dulles, *Revelation Theology*, 29. Dulles has already cited on the issue of the actions of Christ, Augustine's marvelous statement, "Because Christ himself is the Word of God, the very deed of the Word is a word to us" (*Tractates on John* 24, 1).

43. Dulles, *Revelation Theology*, 180.

44. Dulles, *The Craft of Theology*, viii.

45. Avery Dulles, *Magisterium: Teacher and Guardian of the Faith* (Naples, FL: Sapientia Press of Ave Maria University, 2007). One should also note his admiring *The Splendor of Faith: The Theological Vision of Pope John Paul II* (New York: Crossroad Publishing, 1999), which is principally a study of the encyclicals and other magisterial texts produced by that pope, although Wojtyła's personal theology is also considered.

46. Dulles, *The Craft of Theology*, ix.

47. Dulles, *A Testimonial to Grace and Reflections on a Theological Journey*, 50th anniv. ed. (Kansas City, MO: Sheed & Ward, 1996).

48. Dulles, *A Testimonial to Grace*, 131–41.

49. Dulles, *The Craft of Theology*, 6. It is fashionable to call this "anti-foundationalism." Someone in the tradition of the *philosophia perennis* will perhaps want to say that one proposition at least cannot be doubted, namely, that "something exists," a banal statement that, however, can yield on suitable enquiry the mystery of being. If one is sufficiently attuned to Maritain to call that starting point the "intuition of being," then the foundation in question is not strictly propositional, and so the position adopted is not strictly foundationalism.

50. Dulles, *The Craft of Theology*, 6.

51. In *Models of Revelation*, Dulles brackets Polanyi with Newman when describing how, "by arousing the imagination, the affections, and the heuristic impulses, symbols initiate and direct a process whereby the mind, relying partly on unspecifiable clues, perceives radically new patterns and meanings in particular constellations of data" (258).

52. Dulles, *The Craft of Theology*, 8.

53. Dulles, *The Craft of Theology*, 8.

54. Dulles, *The Craft of Theology*, 8.

55. Dulles, *The Craft of Theology*, 9.

56. Dulles, *The Craft of Theology*, 9.

57. Dulles, *The Craft of Theology*, 9.

58. Maurice Blondel, *The Letter on Apologetics and History and Dogma* (New York: Holt, Rinehart and Winston, 1965), 268.

59. Dulles, *The Craft of Theology*, 9.

60. See *The Craft of Theology*, 47, with its appeal to H. R. Niebuhr, *Christ and Culture* (New York: Harper, 1951). Dulles had offered a brief, moderately favorable characterization of the Niebuhr brothers, Reinhold and Helmut Richard, in *Revelation Theology: A History*, 104–5.

61. Dulles, *The Reshaping of Catholicism*, 34–50.

62. Dulles, *The Reshaping of Catholicism*, 39.

63. Dulles, *The Reshaping of Catholicism*, 39–40.

64. Dulles admits the debt of this formulation to the cultural anthropologist Clifford Geertz, notably his *The Interpretation of Cultures* (New York: Basic Books, 1973): thus, *The Reshaping of Catholicism*, 40n2.

65. See especially Joseph Ratzinger, "Faith, Religion, and Culture," in *Truth and Tolerance: Christian Belief and the World Religions*, trans. Henry Taylor (San Francisco: Ignatius Press, 2004), 55–79.

66. Dulles refers to Ary A. Roest Crollius, "Inculturation and the Meaning of Culture," *Gregorianum* 61 (1980): 253–74, which itself drew on David Tracy, "Ethnic Pluralism and Systematic Theology: Reflections," in *Ethnicity*, ed. Andrew M. Greeley and Gregory Baum (New York: Seabury Press, 1977), 91–99.

67. Dulles, *The Reshaping of Catholicism*, 45.

68. Dulles, *The Reshaping of Catholicism*, 45.

69. Dulles, *The Reshaping of Catholicism*, 46.

70. Dulles, *The Reshaping of Catholicism*, 46.

71. Dulles, *The Reshaping of Catholicism*, 47.

72. Dulles, *The Reshaping of Catholicism*, 47–48.

73. Lewis Carroll, *Alice's Adventures in Wonderland and Through the Looking Glass* (New York: Signet Classic, 2000), 35.

74. Johann Adam Möhler, *Die Einheit der Kirche* (Cologne: Olten: Hegner, 1957), 152–53, cited in Dulles, *The Catholicity of the Church*, 78, 126, 152.

2. ENGAGING THE WORLD

1. *Gaudium et Spes*, n. 45. Unless otherwise indicated, Vatican II quotations are taken from *Vatican Council II: The Conciliar and Post Conciliar Documents*,

vol. 1, new rev. ed., ed. Austin Flannery (Northport, NY: Costello Publishing Company, 1996). References to the Council's Dogmatic Constitution on the Church, *Lumen Gentium*, and to *Gaudium et Spes* are indicated by *LG* and *GS*, respectively.

2. See Avery Dulles, *The Dimensions of the Church: A Postconciliar Reflection* (Westminster, MD: Newman, 1967), 73–74.

3. Avery Dulles, *The Reshaping of Catholicism: Current Challenges in the Theology of the Church* (San Francisco: Harper & Row, 1988), 136.

4. See Dulles, *The Reshaping of Catholicism*, 150.

5. Dulles, *The Reshaping of Catholicism*, 150.

6. Avery Dulles, *The Resilient Church: The Necessity and Limits of Adaptation* (Garden City, NY: Doubleday, 1977), 26.

7. Dulles, *The Resilient Church*, 1.

8. Dulles, *The Resilient Church*, 5.

9. Augustine, *Confessions* 7, 10, 16, *Nec tu me in te mutabis, sicut cibum carnis tuae; sed tu mutaberis in me* (PL 32, 742). For the eucharistic interpretation and wide deployment of this text by Henri de Lubac, see Paul McPartlan, *The Eucharist Makes the Church: Henri de Lubac and John Zizioulas in Dialogue*, 2nd ed. (Fairfax, VA: Easter Christian Publications, 2006), 50–74.

10. Dulles, *The Resilient Church*, 5–6.

11. Dulles, *The Resilient Church*, 7.

12. He spoke of *un 'désordre total'*; see the introduction to the chapter by Léon-Joseph Cardinal Suenens, "A Plan for the Whole Council," in *Vatican II by Those Who Were There*, ed. Alberic Stacpoole (London: Geoffrey Chapman, 1986), 88.

13. Gerald P. Fogarty, "The Council Gets Underway," in *History of Vatican II*, vol. 2, ed. G. Alberigo, J. A. Komonchak (Maryknoll, NY: Orbis Books, 1997), 69.

14. Suenens, "A Plan for the Whole Council," 89.

15. See Suenens, "A Plan for the Whole Council," 102–5.

16. Suenens, "A Plan for the Whole Council," 92.

17. Suenens, "A Plan for the Whole Council," 97, see Matt 28:19–20.

18. For Suenens's address, see *Acta Synodalia Sacrosancti Concilii Oecumenici Vaticani II*, vol. I, pt. 4 (Vatican City: Typis Polyglottis Vaticanis, 1971), 222–25; hereafter, *Acta Syn.* I/4.

19. John XXIII, "Radio messaggio di Giovanni XXIII a tutti fedeli cristiani ad un mese dal concilio," September 11, 1962, nos. 6.1–6.3, 6.6, http://www.vatican.va/holy_father/john_xxiii/speeches/1962/documents/hf_j-xxiii_spe_19620911_ecumenical-council_it.html.

20. See *Acta Syn.* I/4, 224–25, 227.

21. See Charles Moeller, "Pastoral Constitution on the Church in the Modern World: History of the Constitution," in *Commentary on the Documents of Vatican II*, vol. 5, ed. Herbert Vorgrimler (New York: Herder and Herder, 1969), 1–76, at 12.

22. See Jan Grootaers, "The Drama Continues between the Acts: The 'Second Preparation' and Its Opponents," in *History of Vatican II*, vol. 2, ed. G. Alberigo, J. A. Komonchak (Maryknoll, NY: Orbis Books, 1997), 366.

23. It is interesting to note that Suenens quoted Matt 28:19 and spoke of the Church's task of evangelization under the heading of the Church *ad intra* in his speech of December 4. *De Ecclesia ad intra* actually referred to all the proper activities of the Church, including mission "in all its aspects." *De Ecclesia ad extra* referred to the Church's response to major problems of the day, for example, poverty, population, war, about which the world was asking it (see *Acta Syn.* I/4, 223–24). *Gaudium et Spes* was initially conceived as a text dealing with such issues but matured into a very weighty text that did indeed deal with specific urgent problems in its second part, but only after a profoundly theological part I, which dealt with the principles that guide the Church's relationship with the world in every age (see *GS* 11–45).

24. Dulles, *The Resilient Church*, 10; quotation from Pope Paul VI, *Evangelii Nuntiandi* (1975), no. 2.

25. See Pope Paul VI, *Ecclesiam Suam* (1964), nos. 96–112.

26. Dulles, *The Dimensions of the Church*, 21–22. He particularly used *Gaudium et Spes* to deal with the latter, namely, the Church's relations with the world of secular life. See *The Dimensions of the Church*, 66–86.

27. Dulles, *The Dimensions of the Church*, 9.

28. See Dulles, *The Dimensions of the Church*, 6–20, 77.

29. Dulles, *The Dimensions of the Church*, 1; See Yves Congar, *Divided Christendom* (London: Geoffrey Bles/The Centenary Press, 1939), 271–73.

30. Henri de Lubac, *Catholicism: Christ and the Common Destiny of Man*, trans. Lancelot C. Sheppard and Elizabeth Englund (San Francisco: Ignatius Press, 1988), 297–98. Dulles refers to de Lubac several times in his own treatment of *The Catholicity of the Church* (Oxford: Clarendon Press, 1985).

31. Dulles, *The Dimensions of the Church*, 3.

32. Dulles, *The Dimensions of the Church*, 14.

33. Dulles, *The Dimensions of the Church*, 78.

34. Dulles, *The Dimensions of the Church*, 10–11.

35. See Dulles, *The Dimensions of the Church*, 27, 31.

36. See Avery Dulles, "The Church, the Churches, and the Catholic Church," *Theological Studies* 33, no. 2 (June 1972): 201: "Exclusivism is particularly prominent in the ecclesiological pronouncements of the Holy See from the middle of the nineteenth century until about 1950, when *Humani generis* [no. 44], with a reference to *Mystici corporis* [1943, no. 13], affirmed that 'The Mystical Body of Christ and the Roman Catholic Church are one and the same thing.'"

37. Dulles, "The Church, the Churches, and the Catholic Church," 210–12, at 212. See Francis A. Sullivan, "Subsistit In," *One in Christ* 22, no. 2 (1986): 115–23.

38. Dulles, "The Church, the Churches, and the Catholic Church," 211.

39. Dulles, "The Church, the Churches, and the Catholic Church," 234.

40. Pope John Paul II, *Ut Unum Sint* (1995), no. 28.

41. Dulles, *The Resilient Church*, 1, 10.

42. See Avery Dulles, *Models of the Church* (New York: Image/Doubleday, 2002), chaps. 2–6. In the second edition of the book, published in 1986, Dulles expanded on the five models described in the first edition of 1974 by adding a chapter on "The Church: Community of Disciples."

43. Dulles, *The Resilient Church*, 24; quotation from Paul VI, *Evangelii Nuntiandi*, no. 14. The encyclical letter continues: "She exists in order to evangelize."

44. Avery Dulles, "Dilemmas Facing the Church in the World," *Origins* 4, no. 35 (February 20, 1975): 549.

45. Dulles, "Dilemmas Facing the Church in the World," 550–51.

46. Dulles, "Dilemmas Facing the Church in the World," 550–51. He adds that, as such, the Church "can give its members a thrilling encounter with the living God."

47. Dulles, *The Resilient Church*, 26.

48. Dulles, *Models of the Church*, 197.

49. See Dulles, *Models of the Church*, 198.

50. 1985 Extraordinary Synod of Bishops, "The Final Report," *Origins* 15, no. 27 (December 19, 1985): 449 (no. II, D, 1). See Avery Dulles, "The Reception of Vatican II at the Extraordinary Synod of 1985," in *The Reception of Vatican II*, ed. Giuseppe Alberigo, Jean-Pierre Jossua, and Joseph A. Komonchak (Washington DC: Catholic University of America, 1987), 355–56.

51. Dulles, *The Reshaping of Catholicism*, 146. Quotations from GS 10, 42, and 58 as given by Dulles.

52. See Congregation for the Doctrine of the Faith, *Doctrinal Note on Some Aspects of Evangelization*, December 3, 2007. See http://www.vatican.va/roman _curia/congregations/cfaith/documents/rc_con_cfaith_doc_20071203_nota -evangelizzazione_en.html.

53. Pope John Paul II, *Redemptoris Missio* (1990), no. 3.

54. See n. 43, above.

55. Avery Dulles, "John Paul II and the New Evangelization," *America* 166, no. 3 (February 1, 1992): 70.

56. See Pope John Paul II, *Redemptoris Missio*, no. 4.

57. Pope John Paul II, *Redemptoris Missio*, no. 55.

58. See Avery Dulles, "Ecumenism and Evangelization," *Origins* 33, no. 23 (November 13, 2003), 400.

59. Pope Paul VI, *Evangelii Nuntiandi*, no. 15; see Dulles, "Ecumenism and Evangelization," 400. In this regard, it is significant that in *Ecclesiam Suam*, when Paul VI described the concentric circles of "The Church in Dialogue," the final and innermost (i.e., fourth) circle comprised Catholics themselves around the pope at the center (see no. 96). He said that he desired that "the Church's internal relationships should take the form of a dialogue between members of a community founded upon love" (no. 114). In other words, he wanted the Church to be in dialogue not only externally but also internally. There was a notable prefiguring of Paul VI's view in Cardinal Suenens's speech to the Council on December 4, 1962. Suenens said that the Council was pursuing a threefold dialogue, the first being dialogue between the Church and its own faithful (*Dialogum Ecclesiae cum fidelibus suis*), the second being ecumenical dialogue, and the third being dialogue with "the world of today" (see *Acta Syn.* I/4, 224).

60. Pope John Paul II, *Redemptoris Missio*, no. 49.

61. See Pope John Paul II, *Redemptoris Missio*, no. 33.

62. Dulles, "Ecumenism and Evangelization," 400.

63. Dulles, "Ecumenism and Evangelization," 402. He continues: "Ecumenical dialogue, so understood, is not primary evangelization but it is pertinent to the kind of continuing evangelization that has been advocated by recent popes."

64. See n. 39.

65. See Dulles, *The Resilient Church*, 26: "Why should the Church strive to become an effective sign or symbol of Christ's presence in the world? I know of no better answer than that which St. Paul gave to a similar question: 'The love of Christ,' he said, 'compels us' (2 Cor 5:14). The Church feels a divine compulsion

to praise and glorify Christ the Lord and to spread the glory of his grace all over the face of the earth."

66. Pope John Paul quotes this verse in *Redemptoris Missio* 1, and goes on to say that the Church's mission "derives not only from the Lord's mandate but also from the profound demands of God's life within us" (no. 11).

67. Dulles, "John Paul II and the New Evangelization," 71, incorporating a quotation from *Redemptoris Missio* 2.

68. Avery Dulles, "Models of Evangelization," *Origins* 37, no. 1 (May 17, 2007): 11.

69. See Avery Dulles, *The Splendor of Faith: The Theological Vision of Pope John Paul II* (New York: Crossroad Publishing, 2003).

70. Avery Dulles, *A History of Apologetics* (San Francisco: Ignatius Press, 1999), xix.

71. Henri de Lubac, *Le fondement théologique des missions* (Paris: Seuil, 1946), 41. De Lubac was reflecting on the meaning of 1 Cor 9:16; for further discussion, see Paul McPartlan, *Sacrament of Salvation* (Edinburgh: T&T Clark, 1995), 72–77.

3. A TALE OF TWO CARDINALS

1. Avery Dulles, *The Craft of Theology: From Symbol to System* (New York: Crossroad Publishing, 1992), 4.

2. Dulles, *The Craft of Theology*, 5.

3. Dulles, *The Craft of Theology*, 5.

4. See Hans-Georg Gadamer, *Truth and Method* (New York: Continuum, 1990), 269–77.

5. See George Lindbeck, *The Nature of Doctrine: Theology in a Postliberal Age* (Philadelphia: Westminster Press, 1984), 34–35.

6. Dulles, *The Craft of Theology*, 6.

7. Dulles, *The Craft of Theology*, 6.

8. Dulles, *The Craft of Theology*, 6.

9. Martha Nussbaum, *Upheavals of Thought: The Intelligence of Emotions* (Cambridge: Cambridge University Press, 2001), esp. 19–49.

10. See John Henry Newman, *An Essay in Aid of a Grammar of Assent* (Notre Dame: University of Notre Dame Press, 1979), 136–37.

11. Newman, *An Essay in Aid of a Grammar of Assent*, 143.

12. Newman, *An Essay in Aid of a Grammar of Assent*, 230.

13. See Robert Barron, *The Priority of Christ: Toward a Postliberal Catholicism* (Grand Rapids, MI: Brazos Press, 2007), 137.

14. Avery Dulles, *Newman* (New York: Continuum, 2002), 44.

15. Dulles, *The Craft of Theology*, 6.

16. John Henry Newman, *An Essay on the Development of Christian Doctrine* (Westminster, MD: Christian Classics, 1968), 36.

17. Newman, *An Essay on the Development of Christian Doctrine*, 40.

18. Newman, *An Essay on the Development of Christian Doctrine*, 34.

19. Dulles, *The Craft of Theology*, 106.

20. Dulles, *The Craft of Theology*, 106.

21. John Henry Newman, *Apologia pro vita sua* (New York: Doubleday, 1956), 323.

22. Dulles, *The Craft of Theology*, 106.

23. Newman, *Apologia pro vita sua*, 328.

24. Newman, *Apologia pro vita sua*, 329.

25. Dulles, *The Craft of Theology*, 106.

26. Newman, *Apologia pro vita sua*, 329.

27. Newman, *Apologia pro vita sua*, 340.

28. Dulles, *The Craft of Theology*, 117.

29. Dulles, *The Craft of Theology*, 117.

30. Dulles, *The Craft of Theology*, 117.

31. Newman, *Apologia pro vita sua*, 340.

32. Dulles, *The Craft of Theology*, 116.

33. Newman, *Apologia pro vita sua*, 339.

34. Dulles, *The Craft of Theology*, 107.

35. Avery Dulles, *A Testimonial to Grace and Reflections on a Theological Journey*, 50th anniv. ed. (Kansas City, MO: Sheed & Ward, 1996), 36.

36. Dulles, *A Testimonial to Grace and Reflections on a Theological Journey*, 132.

4. VATICAN II AND UNDERSTANDING REVELATION

1. I should like to record my gratitude to Father Charles Meyer (professor emeritus for systematic theology at the University of St. Mary of the Lake) for kindly proofreading this article and sharing his comments with me.

2. Donath Hercsik, "Avery Dulles: *Teologo e Cardinale*," *La Civiltà Cattolica* 3 (2003): 357. He had just finished his seminal and award-winning dissertation

on Pico della Mirandola. See Avery Dulles, *Princeps Concordiae: Pico della Mirandola and the Scholastic Tradition*, Harvard Phi Beta Prize Essay for 1940 (Cambridge, MA: University of Harvard Press, 1941). See also A. Dulles, "Umrisse meiner theologischen Methode," in *Entwürfe der Theologie*, ed. Johannes B. Baur (Graz: Styria, 1985), 51. In general, on Dulles's theology, see Dariusz W. Jankiewicz, *The Magisterium and Theologians in the Writings of Avery Robert Dulles* (diss., Ann Arbor, MI: MUI, 2001). Specifically, on Dulles's understanding of revelation, see Thomas Hughson, "Dulles and Aquinas on Revelation," *The Thomist* 52, no. 3 (1988): 445–71; C. F. H. Henry, "The Priority of Revelation," *Journal of the Evangelical Theological Society* 27, no. 1 (1984): 77–92; Ross Allen Schecterle, *Symbolic Mediation, The Theology of Revelation of Avery Dulles, 1980–1993: An Exploration of the Social and Symbolic Dimensions of the Divine Self-Communication* (STL thesis, Leuven University, Belgium, 1994); John F. Russell, *The Development of Theology of Revelation in the United States in the Decade after Dei Verbum: An Analytical and Comparative Study of the Theological Writings of Avery Dulles, S.J. and Gabriel Moran, F.S.C.* (diss., Catholic University of America, Washington, DC, 1978); Francis J. McAree, *Revelation, Faith, and Mystery: The Theology of Revelation in the Writings of Avery Dulles* (diss., Gregorian University, Rome, 1983); David Gordon Poecking, *The Relationship between Faith and Hope in the Recognition of Revelation: An Analysis of the Theology of Avery Dulles, S.J.* (STL thesis, Catholic University of America, Washington, DC, 1996).

    3. He had attended Choate and graduated in 1940 from Harvard in the same class as John F. Kennedy. Before entering the U.S. Navy, he studied for a year and a half at Harvard Law School. In 1946, he was discharged with the rank of a lieutenant. See T. Howland Sanks, "Avery Dulles, 1918-," in *A New Handbook of Christian Theologians*, ed. Donald W. Musser and Joseph L. Price (Nashville, TN: Abingdon Press, 1996), 135–41, at 135.

    4. Avery Dulles, *A Testimonial to Grace and Reflections on a Theological Journey*, 50th anniv. ed. (New York: Sheed & Ward, 1996), 8.

    5. Dulles, *A Testimonial to Grace and Reflections on a Theological Journey*, 4.

    6. Avery Dulles, *Models of Revelation* (Maryknoll, NY: Orbis, 1992), 6–8.

    7. Friedrich Schleiermacher, *The Christian Faith* (Edinburgh: T&T Clark, 1989), para. 9. Emphases added by author.

    8. Dermot Lane, "A Review Essay: Dulles on Revelation," *The Living Light* 21 (October 1984): 74. See "In fact, Dulles' notion of revelation is widely regarded as one of the most developed expressions of…contemporary American Catholic theology" in John R. Connolly, "Revelation as Liberation

from Oppression: Black Theology's Challenge for American Catholic Theology," *Horizons* 26, no. 2 (1999): 232–52, at 234.

9. Dulles has published 23 books and over 750 articles and book reviews. See https://www.fordham.edu/info/24165/mcginley_chair/6829/avery_cardinal_dulles_biography/1 (accessed May 22, 2018).

10. Dulles, "Umrisse meiner theologischen Methode," 52.

11. Dulles, "Umrisse meiner theologischen Methode," 30, 35.

12. Dulles, "Umrisse meiner theologischen Methode," 35–38.

13. Dulles, "Umrisse meiner theologischen Methode," 50.

14. Dulles, *Models of Revelation*, 141–45.

15. Dulles, *A Testimonial to Grace and Reflections on a Theological Journey*, 59–60.

16. Dulles, *A Testimonial to Grace and Reflections on a Theological Journey*, 68.

17. Dulles, *A Testimonial to Grace and Reflections on a Theological Journey*, 97.

18. Plato, *Timaeus, Critias, Cleitophon, Menexenus, Epistles*, Loeb Classical Library 234, trans. R.G. Bury (Cambridge, MA: Harvard University Press, 1929), 37E6–38E6.

19. Dulles, *A Testimonial to Grace and Reflections on a Theological Journey*, 102.

20. He finally wrote his dissertation titled "The Protestant Churches and the Prophetic Office" on an ecumenical topic, the *vestigia ecclesiae*, under the direction of Father Jan Witte, SJ. Unfortunately, it was never published. See Dulles, *A Testimonial to Grace*, 105–6. See also Dulles, "Umrisse meiner theologischen Methode," 54.

21. Dulles, *A Testimonial to Grace and Reflections on a Theological Journey*, 108. This approach developed in contradistinction to the prevailing unquestionable confidence in the tenability of a scientific method defending the rationality of Christian faith, which Dulles termed "historicist apologetics." He had discovered that the Gospels were not history in the strict sense of the word but confessional testimonials.

22. Dulles, "Umrisse meiner theologischen Methode," 59.

23. Avery Dulles, *Models of the Church* (New York: Image Books, Doubleday, 2002).

24. Avery Dulles, *Revelation Theology: A History* (New York: Herder and Herder, 1969).

25. Dulles, *A Testimonial to Grace and Reflections on a Theological Journey*, 127.

26. Dulles, *A Testimonial to Grace and Reflections on a Theological Journey*, 130. Avery Dulles, *The Craft of Theology* (New York: Crossroad, 1995), 105–18, 165–78.

27. As Hercsik succinctly summarizes, *"Considerati in tal modo, i modelli sono una particolare comprensione della realtà e non una comprensione esaustiva della realtà. Infatti, costruendo modelli si procede dal particolare all'universale, dal concreto all'astratto, dall'attuale all'ideale, dal simbolo al sistema. Si tratta di una generalizzazione in cui necessariamente la tipologia di un modello non corrisponde esattamente al pensiero di quanto espresso in altri modelli, perché ogni modello è <complementare> all'altro."* Hercsik, "Avery Dulles: *Teologo e Cardinale*," 359. The term *model* is classical. Aristotle analyzes the typologies of his predecessors in the first book of his *Metaphysics.* The scholastic method employed the genre of *adversarii* to predicate types of schools of thought. However, these approaches did not allow for comparisons of systems from their respective contexts. Thus, it remained a riddle to many a student why someone should be called empiricist, idealist, and so on.

28. Dulles, *The Craft of Theology*, 41–52.

29. Dulles, "Umrisse meiner theologischen Methode," 61.

30. Pierre Rousselot, *Les Yeux de la Foi*, See Rousselot, *Die Augen des Glaubens* (Einsiedeln: Johannes Verlag, 1963). In one single act, one perceives the credibility of faith, both believing and adhering to it simultaneously. It is the fruit of the "lumière de la foi" accessing both faith and reason.

31. Dulles, "Umrisse meiner theologischen Methode," 68.

32. Dulles, *Models of Revelation*, 127–28.

33. Dulles, *Models of Revelation*, 27, 36–52.

34. Dulles, *Models of Revelation*, 27, 53–67.

35. Dulles, *Models of Revelation*, 60.

36. Dulles, *Models of Revelation*, 27 and 68–83.

37. Dulles, *Models of Revelation*, 28 and 84–97.

38. Dulles, *Models of Revelation*, 28.

39. Dulles, *Models of Revelation*, 92.

40. Dulles, *Models of Revelation*, 28, 98–114.

41. Avery Dulles, "Revelation and Discovery," in *Theology and Discovery: Essays in Honor of Karl Rahner, S.J.,* ed. William J. Kelly (Milwaukee, WI: Marquette University Press, 1980), 10–13. See Augustine, *The Confessions of St. Augustine,* trans. Rex Warner (New York: Signet, 2001), bk. 10, chap. 6.

42. Dulles, *Models of Revelation*, 109.

43. Dulles mentions this expression, as does Gadamer, primarily to the (biblical) text and the reader. See Dulles, *Models of Revelation*, 209–10. Hans Georg Gadamer, *Truth and Method* (New York: Crossroad, 1989), 242–54, 302–7.

44. Dulles, *The Craft of Theology*, 30.

45. Avery Dulles, "The Symbolic Structure of Revelation," *Theological Studies* 41, no. 1 (March 1980): 59–60.

46. Dulles, *Models of Revelation*, 131. John Macquarrie, *Principles of Christian Theology* (London: SCM Press, 1966), 104, expresses some unease regarding a direct encounter with the Divine. It cannot be comparable in kind to any other resulting in a personal relationship in the literal sense. Dulles later recalls, "Using the concept of symbolic mediation as a dialectical tool, I attempted to draw maximum value from each of the models and to harmonize them critically." Dulles, *The Craft of Theology*, 50.

47. Gabriel Herman, *Ritualized Friendship and the Greek City* (New York: Cambridge University Press, 1987).

48. Plato, *Symposium*, in *Lysis, Symposium, Gorgias*, Loeb Classical Library 166, trans. W.R.M. Lamb (Cambridge, MA: Harvard University Press, 1925), 191D.

49. An interesting case is the conversion of Marius Victorinus. He was a strict Platonist. Upon realizing that alone he could not be symbolic, he joined Christianity. This insight proved pivotal for Augustine's conversion. See Augustine, *Confessions*, 8, 2, 3–5. Also see A. Solognac, "Le Cercle milanais," in *Les Confessions*, vol. 12, *Œuvres de St. Augustin* (Paris: Desclée, 1962), 529–36. The "We-structure" of Christian faith is essentially symbolic.

50. Karl Rahner developed his understanding of symbol particularly in "The Theology of the Symbol," in *Theological Investigations, vol. IV: More Recent Writings*, trans. Kevin Smyth (London: Darton, Longman and Todd, 1959), 221–52. While there exist in Rahner's views signs, signals, and codes, there are also primary or original symbols, which he terms "*Realsymbol.*" These latter are self-realizations of a being in the other, in a way constitutive of its essence. See Dulles, "The Symbolic Structure of Revelation," 62–68; *Models of Revelation*, 132; *The Craft of Theology*, 20–39, 65. Dulles discovered the significance of symbol around 1966.

51. Mircea Eliade, "Methodological Remarks on the Study of Religious Symbolism," in *The History of Religions*, ed. Mircea Eliade, Joachim Wach, and Joseph M. Kitagawa (Chicago: University of Chicago Press, 1959), 98–103.

52. Dulles, *Models of Revelation*, 132.

53. Dulles, *Models of Revelation*, 136.

54. Dulles, *Models of Revelation*, 148–49.

55. Karl Rahner, *Theological Investigations*, 4:234.

56. Dulles, *The Craft of Theology*, 20.

57. In his opposition to the prevailing positivist interpretation of science, Polanyi argued that it fails to countenance the part that personal commitment and tacit knowledge play in science. Experience exceeds what sense data convey. Even scientific knowledge obtained under rigorous conditions is often tacit in character. Frequently it can only be demonstrated and imitated and transferred in a social system via apprenticeship. In *The Tacit Dimension*, Polanyi writes, "To hold such (scientific) knowledge is an act deeply committed to the conviction that there is something there to be discovered. It is personal, in the sense of involving the personality of him who holds it, and also in the sense of being, as a rule, solitary; but there is no trace of self-indulgence. The discoverer is filled with a compelling sense of responsibility for the pursuit of a hidden truth, which demands his services for revealing it. His act of knowing exercises a personal judgement in relating evidence to an external reality, an aspect of which he is seeking to apprehend" (Michael Polanyi, *The Tacit Dimension* [New York: Anchor, 1967], 24–25). This book is based on the Terry Lectures the author gave at Yale University in 1962. Connoisseurship and criticism are indispensable tools for insight. Serious epistemology must be mindful of such dimensions as commitment and passions as they enable greater knowledge.

58. Dulles, *Models of Revelation*, viii.

59. Thomas Aquinas, *De Veritate*, 12.12. See Thomas Aquinas, *Quaestiones Disputatae de Veritate*, trans. Robert W. Mulligan (Chicago, IL: Regnery, 1952).

60. Dulles, "The Symbolic Structure of Revelation," 60.

61. Heinrich Denzinger, *Enchiridion Symbolorum, Defintionum et Declarationem de Rebus Fiidei et Morum*, 40th ed., ed. Peter Hünermann (Freiburg i. Br: Herder, 2005), no. 3016.

62. John Henry Newman, *An Essay in Aid of a Grammar of Assent* (Notre Dame, IN: University of Notre Dame Press, 2001), esp. 36–48, 270–99.

63. Rahner states, "Symbolic realty is the self-realization of a being in the other," and continues, "Every God-given reality, where it has not been degraded to a purely human tool and to merely utilitarian purposes, states much more than itself: each in its own way is an echo and indication of all reality." Karl Rahner, *Theological Investigations*, 4:234, 239.

64. Dulles, *Models of Revelation*, 131.

65. Polanyi stated, "Things which we can tell, we know by observing them; those that we cannot tell, we know by dwelling in them. All understanding is based on our dwelling in the particulars of that which we comprehend; it is Heidegger's being-in-the-world" (Polányi, *Personal Knowledge* [London: Routledge and Kegan Paul, 1962], x).

66. Dulles, "The Symbolic Structure of Revelation," 60.

67. Avery Dulles, "Faith and Revelation," in *Systematic Theology: Roman Catholic Perspectives*, vol. 1, ed. Francis Schussler Fiorenza and John P. Galvin (Minneapolis: Fortress Press, 1991), 118.

68. Dulles, *The Craft of Theology*, 18ff, 34ff.

69. Dulles, *Models of Revelation*, 138.

70. "*Una realitas complexa*"—Second Vatican Council, "Dogmatic Constitution on the Church," in *Vatican Council II: The Conciliar and Post Conciliar Documents*, ed. Austin Flannery (Northport, NY: Costello Publishing Company, 1996), no. 8.

71. Dulles, *Models of Revelation*, 266–67.

72. Dulles, *Models of Revelation*, 141.

73. Dulles, *Models of Revelation*, 139ff.

74. Dulles, *Models of Revelation*, 136–37. Revelation is not "indefinitely pliable."

75. Dulles *Models of Revelation*, 148–49. The spiritual tension between thematic and unthematic is reminiscent of Rahner's concept of *Vorgriff*—the act of grasping something incomprehensible, or, as Dulles puts it, "anticipatory knowledge that is beyond the 'capacities of conceptual thinking and propositional speech'" (Dulles, *The Craft of Theology*, 18–19). This term intends to convey that one partakes in a reality far greater than one can verbalize. In a terminologically vague but certain way, one becomes aware of the unknowable. See Dulles, "Revelation and Discovery," in *Theology and Discovery: Essays in Honor of Karl Rahner, S.J.*, ed. William J. Kelly (Milwaukee, WI: Marquette University Press, 1980), 9, 13, 20; and Karl Rahner, *Foundations of Christian Faith*, trans. William V. Dych (New York: Crossroad Publishing, 1997), 318–21.

76. Avery Dulles, *A Church to Believe In: Discipleship and the Dynamics of Freedom* (New York: Crossroad Publishing, 1982), 48. Michael Polanyi, "Faith and Reason," *Journal of Religion* 41, no. 4 (October 1961): 237–47; and Polanyi, *Towards a Post-Critical Philosophy* (New York: Harper Torchbooks, 1964).

77. Dulles, *The Craft of Theology*, 66.

78. Dulles, *Models of Revelation*, viii. See also Avery Dulles, "Faith, Church, and God: Insights from Michael Polanyi," *Theological Studies* 45, no. 3 (September 1984): 538.

79. Dulles, *Models of Revelation*, 17.

80. Dulles, "Faith and Revelation," 102–3. See Karl Rahner, *Theological Investigations*, 4:225, 234.

81. Dulles, "Faith and Revelation," 102–3.

82. Dulles, "The Symbolic Structure of Revelation," 73.

83. Dulles, "Faith and Revelation," 101–2.

84. Especially in Dulles, *A Church to Believe In: Discipleship and the Dynamics of Freedom.*

85. George A. Lindbeck, *The Nature of Doctrine: Religion and Theology in a Postliberal Age* (Philadelphia: Westminster, 1984).

86. Dulles, "Faith and Revelation," 121–22.

87. Dulles, *The Reshaping of Catholicism: Current Challenges in the Theology of the Church* (New York: Harper & Row, 1988), 84.

88. Dulles, "Faith and Revelation," 122.

89. John F. Russell, "The Theology of Revelation: Avery Dulles, S.J. and Gabriel Moran," *Irish Theological Quarterly* 54, no. 1 (1988): 25.

90. Dulles, *The Craft of Theology*, 98.

91. Dulles, *The Reshaping of Catholicism*, 84.

92. Dulles, *The Craft of Theology*, 103.

93. Dulles, *The Craft of Theology*, 104.

94. See Russell, "The Theology of Revelation: Avery Dulles, S.J. and Gabriel Moran," 37–38.

95. Athanasius, *De Incarnatione* 54 (New York: Macmillan, 1946), 93.

96. Thomas Aquinas, *Summa Theologiae* (New York: McGraw-Hill, 1964–81), Ia. I. 2.

97. Friedrich Schleiermacher, *On Religion*, trans. R. Couter (Cambridge: Cambridge University Press, 1988), second speech, 133.

98. Paul Tillich, *Systematic Theology* (Chicago: Chicago University Press, 1951), 1:130.

99. Dulles, *Models of Revelation*, 265.

100. Dulles, *Models of Revelation*, 66.

101. See Bernard Lonergan, *Insight: A Study of Human Understanding* (New York: Harper & Row, 1978).

102. Dulles, *Models of Revelation*, 47.

103. See Polanyi, *Personal Knowledge.*

104. Gerald O'Collins, *Interpreting the Resurrection: Examining the Major Problems in the Stories of Jesus' Resurrection* (New York: Paulist Press, 1988).

105. Hercsik, "Avery Dulles: *Teologo e Cardinale*," 369–70.

106. Dulles, *Models of Revelation*, 283.

5. BIBLICAL APOLOGETICS

1. Avery Dulles, *Apologetics and the Biblical Christ* (Westminster, MD: Newman Press, 1966), 4.

2. For further examples, see James L. Kugel, *How to Read the Bible: A Guide to Scripture, Then and Now* (New York: Free Press, 2007).

3. Pius XII, *Divino Afflante Spiritu* (1943), no. 35.

4. Avery Dulles, "Historical Method and the Reality of Christ," in *Church and Society: The McGinley Lectures, 1988–2007* (New York: Fordham University Press, 2008), 103–15.

5. Dulles, *Apologetics and the Biblical Christ*, 31.

6. Dulles, *Apologetics and the Biblical Christ*, 31–32.

7. Dulles, *Apologetics and the Biblical Christ*, 34.

8. Avery Dulles, *A Testimonial to Grace and Reflections on a Theological Journey*, 50th anniv. ed. (Kansas City, MO: Sheed & Ward, 1996), 50–51.

9. Dulles, *Apologetics and the Biblical Christ*, 37–38.

10. Dulles, *Apologetics and the Biblical Christ*, 38.

11. Dulles, *Apologetics and the Biblical Christ*, 39–40.

12. Dulles, *Apologetics and the Biblical Christ*, 45.

13. Dulles, *Apologetics and the Biblical Christ*, 55.

14. Dulles, *Apologetics and the Biblical Christ*, 52.

15. William Albright, *From the Stone Age to Christianity* (Baltimore: Johns Hopkins University Press, 1946), 300.

16. Dulles, *Apologetics and the Biblical Christ*, 72.

17. Dulles, *Apologetics and the Biblical Christ*, 73.

18. Dulles, *Apologetics and the Biblical Christ*, 73.

19. Dulles, *Apologetics and the Biblical Christ*, 73–74.

20. Dulles, "Historical Method and the Reality of Christ," 103–15.

21. Dulles, "Historical Method and the Reality of Christ," 106.

22. Second Vatican Council, "Dogmatic Constitution on Divine Revelation," in *Vatican Council II: The Conciliar and Post Conciliar Documents*, ed. Austin Flannery (Northport, NY: Costello Publishing Company, 1996), no. 19.

23. Dulles, "Historical Method and the Reality of Christ," 110.

24. Dulles, "Historical Method and the Reality of Christ," 111.

6. SHAPING CATHOLIC PRACTICAL THEOLOGY

1. See Avery Dulles, *Models of the Church*, exp. ed. (Garden City, NY: Doubleday, 1987).

2. See Raymond J. Webb, "The Development of a Catholic Practical Theology," *Chicago Studies* 45, no. 1 (Spring 2006); "Catholic Identity: Theology, Practical Theology, and the Catholic College," Hillenmeyer Lecture, Thomas More College, March 21, 2007. A small part of this presentation is drawn from the Hillenmeyer Lecture.

3. Kathleen A. Cahalan, "Beyond Pastoral Theology: Why Catholics Should Embrace Practical Theology" (portions presented at the International Academy of Practical Theology, March 2007, and the Catholic Theological Society of America Practical Theology Group, June 2007), 26, no. 43.

4. Avery Dulles, *Models of Revelation* (Maryknoll, NY: Orbis Books, 1992), 266.

5. Avery, *Models of Revelation*, vii.

6. Avery, *Models of Revelation*, 267.

7. Avery, *Models of Revelation*, 276–78.

8. Avery Dulles, *Apologetics and the Biblical Christ* (Westminster, MD: Newman Press, 1963), ix.

9. Avery Dulles, *The Reshaping of Catholicism* (New York: Harper and Row, 1988), 74.

10. Avery, *The Reshaping of Catholicism*, 91.

11. Richard P. McBrien, *Catholicism* (Minneapolis: Winston, 1980), 1181; quoted in Avery Dulles, *The Catholicity of the Church* (Oxford: Clarendon Press, 1985), 4.

12. Dulles, *The Catholicity of the Church*, 3–4.

13. Extraordinary Synod of Bishops, 1985, Final Report (II.D.1); quoted in Dulles, *The Reshaping of Catholicism*, 195.

14. Avery Dulles, *A Church to Believe In: Discipleship and the Dynamics of Freedom* (New York: Crossroad Publishing, 1982), 7–14.

15. Dulles, *The Reshaping of Catholicism*, 28.

16. Avery Cardinal Dulles, "Can the Laity Properly Be Called 'Ministers'?" *Origins* 35, no. 44 (April 20, 2006): 725–31; *A Church to Believe In*, 12.

17. Avery Dulles, *A Testimonial to Grace and Reflections on a Theological Journey*, 50th anniv. ed. (Kansas City, MO: Sheed & Ward, 1996), 105–6.

18. Dulles, *A Testimonial to Grace and Reflections on a Theological Journey*, 30.

19. Avery Dulles, *The Craft of Theology* (New York: Crossroad Publishing, 1992), 17–21; cf. George Lindbeck, *The Nature of Doctrine* (Philadelphia: Westminster, 1984), 10–22.

20. See Miroslav Volf and Dorothy C. Bass, eds., *Practicing Theology: Beliefs and Practices in Christian Life* (Grand Rapids, MI: W.B. Eerdmans, 2002).

21. Dulles, *The Catholicity of the Church*, 6–7.

22. Webb, "The Development of a Catholic Practical Theology," 110.

23. Avery Dulles, "Philosophy and Priestly Formation," *Theology Digest* 50, no. 4 (Winter 2003): 345; Dulles, *The Reshaping of Catholicism*, 195; and Dulles, *The Craft of Theology*, 126–29.

24. Dulles, *The Craft of Theology*, 154–55.

25. Dulles, *The Craft of Theology*, 155.

26. Dulles, *The Craft of Theology*, 156.

27. Dulles, *The Craft of Theology*, 157.

28. Dulles, *The Craft of Theology*, 159.

29. Dulles, *The Craft of Theology*, 159.

30. Dulles, *The Craft of Theology*, 22.

31. Dulles, *The Craft of Theology*, 24.

32. Dulles, *The Craft of Theology*, 25.

33. Dulles, *The Craft of Theology*, 24.

34. Dulles, *A Church to Believe In*, 125.

35. Dulles, *The Craft of Theology*, 129–30.

36. Dulles, *A Testimonial to Grace and Reflections on a Theological Journey*, 127.

37. Dulles, "Philosophy and Priestly Formation," 344.

38. Avery Dulles, "Theological Education in Jesuit Formation," *Review for Religious*, 59, no. 3 (2000): 238.

39. Dulles, *The Reshaping of Catholicism*, 166–67.

40. Dulles, "Theological Education in Jesuit Formation," 239–40.

41. Avery Dulles, "Prospects for Seminary Theology," *Seminary Journal* 2, no. 3 (Winter 1996): 17.

42. Dulles, "Prospects for Seminary Theology," 14.

43. Avery Dulles, *The History of Apologetics* (New York: Corpus Books, 1971).

44. Avery Dulles, "The Catholic Press and the New Evangelization," *Origins* 27, no. 4 (June 12, 1997): 62.

45. Avery Dulles, "Models of Evangelization," *Origins* 37, no. 1 (May 17, 2007): 8–12.

46. Dulles, *Craft of Theology*, 47.

47. Dulles, *A Testimony to Grace and Reflections on a Theological Journey*, 119.

48. Dulles, *Models of Revelation*, preface.

49. See Avery Dulles, *The Assurance of Things Hoped For: A Theology of Christian Faith* (New York: Oxford University Press, 1994), 177–79.

50. Avery Dulles, "Theological Education in the Catholic Tradition," in *Theological Education in the Catholic Tradition*, ed. Patrick W. Carey and Earl C. Muller (New York: Crossroad Publishing, 1997), 18–19; cf. Joseph A. Komonchak, "Recapturing the Great Tradition: In Memoriam Henri de Lubac," *Commonweal* 119, no. 2 (January 31, 1992): 14–17.

51. Avery Cardinal Dulles, "Farewell Address as McGinley Professor," in *The Legacy of Avery Cardinal Dulles, S.J.: His Words and His Witness*, ed. Anne-Marie Kirmse and Michael M. Canaris (New York: Fordham University Press, 2011), 101–2.

CONCLUSION:
FROM CONVERT TO CARDINAL

1. Avery Dulles, "Coming Home," in *Where I Found Christ*, ed. John A. O'Brien (Garden City, NJ: Doubleday and Company, 1950), 66.

2. "Harvard as an Invitation to Catholicism," in *The Catholics of Harvard Square*, ed. Jeffrey Wills (Petersham, MA: St. Bede's Publications, 1993), 120.

3. Avery Dulles, "Heresy Today?" *America* 142, no. 8 (March 1, 1980): 163.

4. Avery Dulles, *Models of Revelation* (Garden City, NY: Doubleday and Company, 1983), vii–xi.

5. Dulles, *Models of Revelation*, 35.

6. The influence of scientists such as Ian Barbour, I. T. Ramsey, and Michael Polanyi can be seen in Dulles's exploration of models.

7. Dulles, *Models of Revelation*, 30.

8. Avery Dulles, *Models of the Church* (Garden City, NY: Doubleday and Company, 1974), 21.

9. Dulles, *Models of the Church*, 22.

10. Dulles, *Models of Revelation*, 30.

11. In this, he is following in the tradition of Ernst Troeltsch and H. R. Niebuhr, and is in sharp contradistinction with David Tracy, who holds that models represent mutually incompatible options.

12. Dulles, *Models of the Church*, 9.

13. Dulles, *Models of the Church*, 186.

14. Avery Dulles, *The Resilient Church* (Garden City, NY: Doubleday and Company, 1977), 26.

15. Avery Dulles, *A Church to Believe In: Discipleship and the Dynamics of Freedom* (New York: Crossroad Publishing, 1982), 46.

16. Dulles, *A Church to Believe In*, 5.

17. See Dulles, *A Church to Believe In*, chap. 1, "Imaging the Church for the 1980's," 1–18, for a more detailed treatment of this topic.

18. Dulles, *A Church to Believe In*, 5.

19. Dulles, *A Church to Believe In*, 17–18.

20. Dulles, *A Church to Believe In*, 3.

21. Dulles, *A Church to Believe In*, 4–6.

22. Avery Dulles, *The Reshaping of Catholicism* (San Francisco: Harper & Row, 1988), 26.

23. Peter Steinfels, "Fordham's New Theologian: A Flair for Diplomacy," *New York Times*, October 2, 1988, sect. 1. See https://www.nytimes.com/1988/10/02/nyregion/fordham-s-new-theologian-a-flair-for-diplomacy.html.

24. Dulles, *The Resilient Church*, 2.

25. Avery Dulles, "Vatican II and the Church's Purpose," *Theology Digest* 32, no. 4 (Winter 1985): 345.

26. Dulles, "Vatican II and the Church's Purpose," 349.

27. Dulles, "Vatican II and the Church's Purpose," 349–50.

28. Steinfels, "Fordham's New Theologian: A Flair for Diplomacy."

29. Dulles, "Vatican II and the Church's Purpose," 351.

30. Avery Dulles, "Paths to Doctrinal Agreement," *Theological Studies* 47, no. 1 (1986): 46–47.

31. Dulles, *The Resilient Church*, 171.

32. Dulles, *A Church to Believe In*, 102.

BIBLIOGRAPHY

CHURCH DOCUMENTS

1985 Extraordinary Synod of Bishops. "The Final Report." *Origins* 15, no. 27 (1985): 444–50.

Acta Synodalia Sacrosancti Concilii Oecumenici Vaticani II. Vol. 1, pt. 4. Typis Polyglottis Vaticanis, 1971.

Pope John XXIII. "Radio messaggio a tutti fedeli cristiani ad un mese dal concilio." September 11, 1962. http://w2.vatican.va/content/john -xxiii/it/speeches/1962/documents/hf_j-xxiii_spe_19620911 _ecumenical-council.html.

Pope John Paul II. *Redemptoris Missio.* Rome: Libreria Editrice Vaticana, 1990.

———. *Ut Unum Sint.* Rome: Libreria Editrice Vaticana, 1995.

Pope Paul VI. *Ecclesiam Suam.* Rome: Libreria Editrice Vaticana, 1964.

———. *Evangelii Nuntiandi.* Rome: Libreria Editrice Vaticana, 1975.

Pope Pius XII. *Divino Afflante Spiritu.* Rome: Libreria Editrice Vaticana, 1943.

Second Vatican Council. "Dogmatic Constitution on Divine Revelation." In *Vatican Council II: The Conciliar and Post Conciliar Documents*, edited by Austin Flannery, 750–65. Northport, NY: Costello Publishing, 1996.

———. *Vatican Council II: The Conciliar and Post Conciliar Documents.* Vol. 1, new rev. ed. Edited by Austin Flannery. Northport, NY: Costello Publishing, 1996.

WORKS BY AVERY DULLES, SJ

Dulles, Avery. *Apologetics and the Biblical Christ.* Westminster, MD: Newman Press, 1963.

———. *Apologetics and the Biblical Christ.* London: Burns & Oates, 1964.

———. *The Assurance of Things Hoped For: A Theology of Christian Faith.* New York: Oxford University Press, 1994.

———. "Can the Laity Properly Be Called 'Ministers'?" *Origins* 35, no. 44 (2006): 725–31.

———. *The Catholicity of the Church.* Oxford: Clarendon Press, 1985.

———. "The Catholic Press and the New Evangelization." *Origins* 27, no. 4 (1997): 62–63.

———. *A Church to Believe In: Discipleship and the Dynamics of Freedom.* New York: Crossroad Publishing, 1982.

———. "The Church, the Churches, and the Catholic Church." *Theological Studies* 33, no. 2 (1972): 199–234.

———. "Coming Home." In *Where I Found Christ*, edited by John A. O'Brien, 63–81. Garden City, NY: Doubleday and Company, 1950.

———. *The Craft of Theology: From Symbol to System.* Dublin: Gill and Macmillan, 1992.

———. *The Craft of Theology: From Symbol to System.* New York: Crossroad Publishing, 1995.

———. "Dilemmas Facing the Church in the World." *Origins* 4, no. 35 (1975): 548–51.

———. *The Dimensions of the Church: A Postconciliar Reflection.* Westminster, MD: Newman Press, 1967.

———. "Ecumenism and Evangelization." *Origins* 33, no. 23 (2003): 399–402.

———. "Faith and Revelation." In *Systematic Theology: Roman Catholic Perspectives*, vol. 1, edited by Francis Schussler Fiorenza and John P. Galvin, 89–128. Minneapolis: Fortress Press, 1991.

———. "Farewell Address as McGinley Professor." In *The Legacy of Avery Cardinal Dulles, S.J.: His Words and His Witness*, edited by Anne-Marie Kirmse and Michael M. Canaris, 96–102. New York: Fordham University Press, 2011.

————. "Harvard as an Invitation to Catholicism." In *The Catholics of Harvard Square*, edited by Jeffrey Wills, 119–24. Petersham, MA: St. Bede's Publications, 1993.

————. "Heresy Today?" *America* 142, no. 8 (1980): 162–64.

————. "Historical Method and the Reality of Christ." In *Church and Society: The McGinley Lectures, 1988–2007*, 103–15. New York: Fordham University Press, 2008.

————. *A History of Apologetics*. San Francisco: Ignatius Press, 1999.

————. "John Paul II and the New Evangelization." *America* 166, no. 3 (1992): 52–59, 69–72.

————. "Models of Evangelization." *Origins* 37, no. 1 (2007): 8–12.

————. *Models of the Church*. New York: Doubleday and Company, 1974.

————. *Models of the Church*. Expanded ed. New York: Image Books, Doubleday, 2002.

————. *Models of Revelation*. Garden City, NY: Doubleday, 1983.

————. *Models of Revelation*. Maryknoll, NY: Orbis Books, 1992.

————. *Newman*. New York: Continuum, 2002.

————. "Paths to Doctrinal Agreement." *Theological Studies* 47, no. 1 (1986): 32–47.

————. "Philosophy and Priestly Formation." *Theology Digest* 50, no. 4 (2003): 343–52.

————. *Princeps Concordiae: Pico della Mirandola and the Scholastic Tradition*. Cambridge, MA: Harvard University Press, 1941.

————. "Prospects for Seminary Theology." *Seminary Journal* 2, no. 3 (Winter 1996): 12–19.

————. *The Reshaping of Catholicism: Current Challenges in the Theology of the Church*. New York: Harper & Row, 1988.

————. *The Resilient Church: The Necessity and Limits of Adaptation*. Garden City, NY: Doubleday, 1977.

————. "Revelation and Discovery." In *Theology and Discovery: Essays in Honor of Karl Rahner, SJ*, edited by William J. Kelly, 1–29. Milwaukee, WI: Marquette University Press, 1980.

————. *Revelation Theology: A History*. London: Burns & Oates, 1970.

————. "The Symbolic Structure of Revelation." *Theological Studies* 41, no. 1 (1980): 51–73.

————. *A Testimonial to Grace and Reflections on a Theological Journey*, 50th. anniv. ed. Kansas City, MO: Sheed & Ward, 1996.

————. "Theological Education in Jesuit Formation." *Review for Religious* 59, no. 3 (2000): 230–40.

————. "Theological Education in the Catholic Tradition." In *Theological Education in the Catholic Tradition*, edited by Patrick W. Carey and Earl C. Muller, 10–22. New York: Crossroad Publishing, 1997.

————. "Umrisse meiner theologischen Methode." In *Entwürfe der Theologie*, edited by Johannes B. Baur, 51–70. Graz, Austria: Styria, 1985.

————. "Vatican II and the Church's Purpose." *Theology Digest* 32, no. 4 (1985): 341–52.

OTHER WORKS

Adiprasetya, Joas. "George A. Lindbeck and Postliberal Theology." *Boston Collaborative Encyclopedia of Modern Western Theology*, 2005. http://people.bu.edu/wwildman/bce/mwt_themes_862_lindbeck.htm#George_A._Lindbeck_and_Postliberal_Theology_.

Albright, William. *From the Stone Age to Christianity*. Baltimore: Johns Hopkins University Press, 1946.

Aquinas, Thomas. *Quaestiones Disputatae de Veritate*. Translated by Robert W. Mulligan. Chicago: Regnery, 1952.

————. *Summa Theologiae*. New York: McGraw-Hill, 1964–81.

Athanasius. *De Incarnatione*, 54. New York: Macmillan, 1946.

Augustine. *Confessions*. PL 32.

Baima, Thomas A. "The Use of Heuristic Theory in the Study of the Evangelical Lutheran Church in America." Paper presented at the Midwest American Academy of Religion, Chicago, Illinois, April 6, 2002.

Barth, Karl. *Church Dogmatics*. Vol. 1, pt. 1. Edinburgh: T&T Clark, 1936.

Blondel, Maurice. *The Letter on Apologetics and History and Dogma*. New York: Holt, Rinehart and Winston, 1965.

Cahalan, Kathleen A. "Beyond Pastoral Theology: Why Catholics Should Embrace Practical Theology." Portions presented at the International

Academy of Practical Theology, March 2007, and the Catholic Theological Society of America Practical Theology Group, June 2007.

Carroll, Lewis. *Alice's Adventures in Wonderland and Through the Looking Glass*. New York: Signet Classic, 2000.

Cousins, Ewert. "Models and the Future of Theology." *Continuum* 7 (1969): 78–91.

de Lubac, Henri. *Catholicism: A Study of Dogma in Relation to the Corporate Destiny of Mankind*. London: Burns, Oates and Washbourne, 1950.

————. *Catholicism: Christ and the Common Destiny of Man*. Translated by Lancelot C. Sheppard and Elizabeth Englund. San Francisco: Ignatius Press, 1988.

————. *Le fondement théologique des missions*. Paris: Éditions du Seuil, 1946.

Denzinger, Heinrich. *Enchiridion Symbolorum, Defintionum et Declarationem de Rebus Fiidei et Morum*, 40th ed., edited by Peter Hünermann. Freiburg i. Br: Herder, 2005.

Fogarty, Gerald P. "The Council Gets Underway." In *History of Vatican II*, vol. 2, edited by G. Alberigo and J.A. Komonchak, 69–106. Maryknoll, NY: Orbis Books, 1997.

Gadamer, Hans Georg. *Truth and Method*. New York: Crossroad Publishing, 1989.

Grootaers, Jan. "The Drama Continues between the Acts: The 'Second Preparation' and Its Opponents." In *History of Vatican II*, vol. 2, edited by G. Alberigo & J.A. Komonchak, 359–514. Maryknoll, NY: Orbis Books, 1997.

Hammond, John S., Ralph L. Keeney, and Howard Raiffa. "The Hidden Traps in Decision Making." *Harvard Business Review* 76, no. 5 (1998): 47–58.

Hercsik, Donath. "Avery Dulles: Teologo e Cardinale." *La Civiltà Cattolica* 3 (2003): 357–70.

Küng, Hans. *My Struggle for Freedom: Memoirs*. Grand Rapids, MI: William B. Eerdmans Publishing, 2002.

Kushiner, James M., et al. "Plausible Ecumenism: An Ecumenical Roundtable Discussion." *Touchstone* 13, no. 1 (2000): 21–42.

Lane, Dermot. "A Review Essay: Dulles on Revelation." *The Living Light* 21 (1984): 74–76.

Macquarrie, John. *Principles of Christian Theology*. London: SCM Press, 1966.

McBrien, Richard P. *Catholicism*. Minneapolis: Winston, 1980.

———. *Church: The Continuing Quest*. New York: Newman Press, 1970.

Newman, John Henry. *Apologia pro vita sua*. New York: Doubleday, 1956.

———. *An Essay in Aid of a Grammar of Assent*. Notre Dame, IN: University of Notre Dame Press, 1979/2001.

———. *An Essay on the Development of Christian Doctrine*. Westminster, MD: Christian Classics, 1968.

———. *Newman's University Sermons: Fifteen Sermons Preached before the University of Oxford, 1826–1843*. 3rd ed. London: Society for Promoting Christian Knowledge, 1970.

Nussbaum, Martha. *Upheavals of Thought: The Intelligence of Emotions*. Cambridge: Cambridge University Press, 2001.

Plato. *Lysis, Symposium, Gorgias*. Loeb Classical Library 166. Translated by W.R.M. Lamb. Cambridge, MA: Harvard University Press, 1925.

———. *Timaeus, Critias, Cleitophon, Menexenus, Epistles*. Loeb Classical Library 234. Translated by R.G. Bury. Cambridge, MA: Harvard University Press, 1929.

Polanyi, Michael. *Personal Knowledge*. London: Routledge and Kegan Paul, 1962.

———. *The Tacit Dimension*. New York: Anchor, 1967.

Pozzo, Guido. "Method: Systematic Theology." In *Dictionary of Fundamental Theology*, edited by René Latourelle and Rino Fisichella, 670–84. New York: Crossroad Publishing, 1994.

Rahner, Karl. *Theological Investigations, vol. IV, More Recent Writings*. Translated by Kevin Smyth. London: Darton, Longman and Todd, 1959.

Rousselot, Pierre. *The Eyes of Faith and Answer to Two Attacks*. Translated by John M. McDermott and Avery Dulles. New York: Fordham University Press, 1991.

Russell, John F. "The Theology of Revelation: Avery Dulles, S.J. and Gabriel Moran." *Irish Theological Quarterly* 54, no. 1 (1988): 21–40.

Russo, J. Edward, and Paul J. H. Schoemaker. *Decision Traps: The Ten Barriers to Brilliant Decision-Making and How to Overcome Them.* New York: Simon & Schuster, 1989.

Sanks, T. Howland. "Avery Dulles, 1918–." In *A New Handbook of Christian Theologians,* edited by Donald W. Musser, Joseph L. Price, 135–41. Nashville: Abingdon Press, 1996.

Schleiermacher, Friedrich. *The Christian Faith.* Edinburgh: T&T Clark, 1989.

———. *On Religion.* Translated by R. Couter. Cambridge: Cambridge University Press, 1988.

Steinfels, Peter. "Fordham's New Theologian: A Flair for Diplomacy." *New York Times,* October 2, 1988, sect. 1.

Suenens, Léon–Joseph Cardinal. "A Plan for the Whole Council." In *Vatican II by Those Who Were There,* edited by Alberic Stacpoole, 88–105. London: Geoffrey Chapman, 1986.

Tillich, Paul. *Systematic Theology.* Vol. 1. Chicago: Chicago University Press, 1951.

Webb, Raymond J. "Catholic Identity: Theology, Practical Theology, and the Catholic College." Hillenmeyer Lecture, Thomas More College, March 21, 2007.

———. "The Development of a Catholic Practical Theology." *Chicago Studies* 45, no. 1 (2006): 105–17.

Willimon, William H. *What's Right with the Church.* New York: Harper & Row, 1985.

CONTRIBUTORS

Thomas A. Baima
The Very Reverend Thomas A. Baima is a priest of the Archdiocese of Chicago, Vice Rector for Academic Affairs of the University of Saint Mary of the Lake, and professor of dogmatic theology. He is also Vicar for Ecumenical and Interreligious Affairs of the Archdiocese of Chicago. (STD, Pontifical University of Saint Thomas Aquinas in Rome)

Robert Barron
The Most Reverend Robert E. Barron is Auxiliary Bishop of Los Angeles and founder of Word on Fire Catholic Ministries. As a priest of the Archdiocese of Chicago, he served as Rector/President of the University of Saint Mary of the Lake/ Mundelein Seminary and Francis Cardinal George Professor of Faith and Culture. (STD, Institut Catholique de Paris)

Emery de Gaál
The Reverend Emery de Gaál is a priest of the Diocese of Eichstad in Bavaria and professor of dogmatic theology at the University of Saint Mary of the Lake. (PhD, Duquesne University)

Anne-Marie Kirmse, OP
Dominican Sister Anne-Marie Kirmse served as Avery Dulles's Research Associate and Executive Assistant for his twenty years at Fordham University. Since the cardinal's death in 2008, she continues at Fordham as Research Associate for

the McGinley Chair and as Associate Professor of Theology in the College of Liberal Studies. (PhD, Fordham University)

Paul McPartlan

The Reverend Monsignor Paul McPartlan is a priest of the Archdiocese of Westminster, Ordinary Professor of Historical and Systematic Theology and Carl J. Peter Professor of Systematic Theology and Ecumenism at the Catholic University of America. (DPhil, University of Oxford)

Aidan Nichols, OP

The Reverend Aidan Nichols is a priest of the Order of Friars Preacher. He was the first John Paul II Memorial Visiting Lecturer at the University of Oxford and is former prior and current subprior of the Priory of Saint Michael the Archangel at the University of Cambridge. (PhD, University of Edinburgh)

Edward T. Oakes, SJ

The Late Reverend Edward T. Oakes was a priest of the Society of Jesus, Chester and Margaret Paluch Professor of Theology, and professor of dogmatic theology at the University of Saint Mary of the Lake. He previously taught on the faculties of Regis University and New York University. (PhD, Union Theological Seminary)

Raymond J. Webb

The Reverend Raymond J. Webb is a priest of the Archdiocese of Chicago, former Academic Dean, and professor of pastoral theology at the University of Saint Mary of the Lake. He previously served on the faculty of Niles College of Loyola University Chicago. (PhD, Loyola University Chicago)

INDEX

Index